AF480628

THE INVISIBLE CLEARLY SEEN

THE INVISIBLE CLEARLY SEEN

Tracing Biblical Symbols in Creation

Benjamin Marshall

The Invisible Clearly Seen
Tracing Biblical Symbols in Creation

Benjamin Marshall

Bible quotations that have text rendered in italics are for emphasis that the author of this book intends.

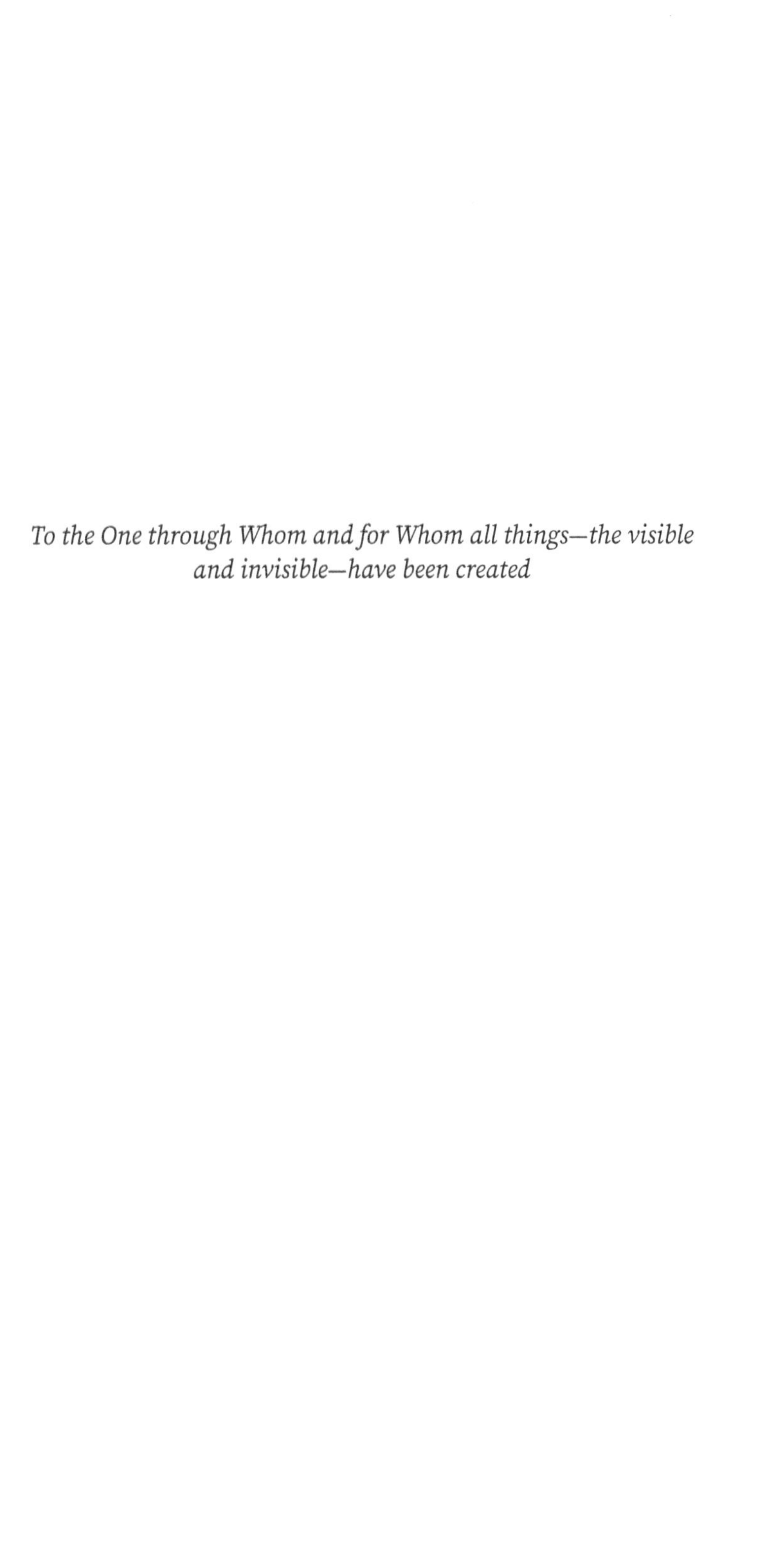

To the One through Whom and for Whom all things—the visible and invisible—have been created

Introduction

You can't open your eyes in this universe without seeing a theater of divine revelation.

R. C. Sproul

I think I'm quite ready for another adventure.

Bilbo Baggins

The veil between the mundane and the miraculous is an illusion.

The trees of the forest shout for joy (Psalm 96:12). The rivers clap their hands (Psalm 98:8). The mountains break into singing and the rocks cry out (Isaiah 55:12; Luke 19:40).

Can you hear it?

Logical Beauty & Beautiful Logic

In Genesis 1, God brings order from formlessness. Physical reality, as we know it, is exquisitely crafted during the six days of creation. God speaks cycles of nature, mathematics, and time into existence. We would describe the result as logical. As humans, hand-crafted in the *Imago Dei* and placed into creation, we are able to discover and understand the logic infused into the world. It is, however, not only a logical world but a magnificently beautiful one.

The physical world contains beauty that we can see, hear, smell, taste, and touch. One can surmise that God could have made a grayscale world—a world where we could only hear between 200–2000 Hz, eat only grass, and smell nothing. But (gratefully), He did not! When He spoke His handiwork into being, it was stunningly beautiful.

The artistry of our world evidences the Artist.

> The heavens declare the glory of God,
> and the sky proclaims the work of His hands.
> Day after day they pour out speech;
> night after night they communicate knowledge.
> There is no speech; there are no words;
> their voice is not heard.
> Their message has gone out to all the earth,
> and their words to the ends of the world.
> (Psalm 19:1–4)

Though lacking vocal chords, creation's proclamation goes forth. The Creator's "invisible attributes, that is, His eternal power and divine nature, have been clearly seen since the creation of the world, being understood through what He has made" (Romans 1:20).

Can you see it?

In creation, there are elements that have consistent meaning throughout human existence—"archetypes," if you will. These are uncanny patterns with consistent imagery and meanings that appear to be embedded into creation and even the human psyche.[1]

The themes we shall explore in the following pages can be found in creation—whether nature or human nature. That being the case, they are both logical. . . and beautiful! They are logical in that these are clear patterns that form coherent thoughts and meanings. They are beautiful in that these symbols are readily found all around us.

These thematic symbols were not, however, chosen only because they can be observed in the natural world. First and foremost, these nine themes were chosen because they are *in the Bible*.

Seen even from a pagan perspective, the Bible is a literary masterpiece.

The book of Jonah is considered a book of satirical brilliance. Jesus routinely used hyperbole to stress points in His teachings. Just in the Sermon on the Mount, Jesus uses questions such as, "If your right eye causes you to sin, gouge it out" and "Why do you look at the speck in your brother's eye but don't notice the log in your own eye?" (Matthew 5:29; 7:3). Song of Songs is a chiastic poem filled with rich imagery. There are many different genres of writing with countless examples of literary devices—symbolism being but one example.

Jesus Himself references Jonah in the belly of the great fish for three days as a foreshadowing metaphor of the three days He would be in the tomb (Matthew 12:40). Peter references Noah and the great flood as a metaphor for baptism (1 Peter 3:20–21). John utilizes a single-word metaphor, "Word," to introduce Jesus in his gospel—connecting Jesus to Genesis 1, while illustrating His preeminence, divinity, and His being the Word of salvation.

Jesus taught that wildflowers remind us not to worry, that the

---

1   For our purposes, terms such as *archetype, symbol, motif,* and *theme* will all be used interchangeably.

wind teaches us about the Spirit (John 3:7–8), and that lightning should cause us to exclaim, "Maranatha!" (see Matthew 24:27 and 1 Corinthians 16:22).

If God's living Word makes use of such metaphoric imagery, should we not pay more attention to these patterns?

Charting the Course

Let us take a moment to clarify what this exploration through Scriptural symbols is *not* about.

Firstly, this work contains no numerology. While there are sections discussing important numbers in the Bible, we will not be trying to apply some mystical relationship between numbers and your destiny or current events. There certainly will not be any predictions as to the timing of eschatological events—for only the Father knows these days and times.

Secondly, the hope is to remain theologically consistent. Context is very much our friend when we pore over the pages of Scripture. There are many instances in the Bible of metaphor, poetry, symbolism, parable, hyperbole, typology, prophecy, and other contextual literary facets. Even so, we want to focus on themes that are *consistent* and *frequent* and, of course, that fit agreeably within the greater truths in the Scriptures.

As mentioned earlier, the chief reason for picking these particular themes is that they are in Scripture. We will seek to start with the source (the Bible) rather than looking to extra-biblical patterns and attempting to apply them to the Bible. We will not be trying to overlay Jungian archetypes, personality types, or other such things on top of the Scriptures. Although there are certainly metaphors in the world that fit nicely with Scripture (an example is Jonathan Edwards using the silkworm as metaphor for Christ), we shall—as much as possible—avoid laying on any extra-biblical themes.

Finally, these nine topics are certainly not an exhaustive list of the symbols used throughout the Bible. Even within these themes, there are many more ways in which they show themselves. No doubt, there are greater depths of meanings that may be gleaned and additional applications to one's life.

How to Read this Book

This book has been divided into two sections.

Part one is the bulk of the book—the nine thematic explorations through Scripture. With each of these themes, we shall briefly analyze the generally accepted views on their symbolic meanings throughout human history. We will then look at the biblical symbolism and go on an adventure—from Genesis to Revelation—to uncover patterns, interpretations, and relevant applications to our lives.

Part two is the "grand finale," showcasing all the themes coming together. Indeed, there is a section of the Bible where *all of these symbols appear together!*

How awesome is that? It blew my mind the first time I read it. In fact, I think it is so spectacular that I will not even reference this passage of Scripture until the concluding part of the book.

As you read, might I suggest that you go out into creation. Find a peaceful park bench, lie on the beach, or sit next to a babbling brook. You will, hopefully, begin to "put on new lenses" and see some of these symbols all around you.

I would also humbly suggest that you, the reader, should prayerfully ponder this information. Ruminate on these truths and their applications to your life.

There are *quite a few* biblical quotes and Scripture references. This is for several reasons, mainly:

1. To validate the premise that these themes are woven into the Bible from cover to cover.
2. To reference enough of the source text (the Bible) in context so that readers are not required to keep a Bible handy at all times while venturing through these thematic explorations and,
3. God's words will always be more powerful than mine. His words never return to Him empty or fail to accomplish what He pleases (Isaiah 55:11).

Even so, it is my recommendation that you read through the expanded Scripture references. There is simply not enough room to include every relevant piece of Scripture or the full passages that are referenced. Readers are encouraged to explore these and, of course, to discover their own adventures through God's living Word.

Ultimately, my prayer and aim is that this book fulfills the following goals. . .

Reinforce the Congruence of Scripture

The Bible contains sixty-six books written in three languages over the course of about 1,500 years by forty different authors across three continents.[2] In 2007, Chris Harrison and Pastor Christoph Römhild indexed a dataset of 63,779 cross references found in the Bible (a "cross reference" is when the Bible "quotes itself" either directly or through phrases or subject matter). They then put together a work of art visually displaying all the internal biblical connections.[3]

When I see amazing work like this, I see God's breath all over the pages of Scripture (2 Timothy 3:16). There is simply no way these different authors, with different backgrounds, in different locales, perfectly coordinated all of these threads. These themes are yet another layer displaying divine inspiration. I pray that the following adventures further reinforce the divine continuity of Scripture.

Hiding the Word in Our Hearts

The psalmist speaks of "hiding" or "treasuring" God's Word in our hearts. This is the spiritual discipline of Scripture study and memory.

In the award-winning television series, *Sherlock*, featuring Benedict Cumberbatch as Sherlock Holmes, the actor faces an arch-nemesis who utilizes his extraordinary memory skills to

---

2 The number of authors can depend on whom we attribute some of the writings to—such as the Letter to the Hebrews. However, the point remains.

3 To view their amazing work, visit: https://www.chrisharrison.net/index.php/visualizations/BibleViz

frustrate the sleuth. The diabolical mastermind describes this technique as his "mind palace" where he can go and retrieve information on anyone he chooses—including Sherlock.

This is, in fact, a real concept and falls under the category of mnemonics. A mnemonic device is a learning technique that aids in the retention or retrieval in the human memory. There are many different examples of these "tricks" helping humans memorize fantastic amounts of information.

I have personally found, and hope you do as well, that these symbols woven through Scripture aid in memorizing the Word. Since most of these symbols are found in the physical world, even looking at a campfire or taking in a sunrise can become "mnemonic devices" that bring these connected Scriptures to mind.

May We See the Divine in the World Around Us
(Awareness—Attention—Awe)

Awareness

Perspective is a funny thing.

We humans can eat without really tasting, hear without really listening, and look without really perceiving. "Between the emotion and the response falls the shadow."[4]

Sometimes, we are not aware because we simply do not know. The Lord's case against Israel in Hosea is: "There is no truth, no faithful love, and no knowledge of God in the land!" (Hosea 4:1). Let us strive to know and love our Lord! As the great preacher Charles Spurgeon said, "Nobody ever outgrows Scripture; the book widens and deepens with our years."

Our perspective is also warped because we are in the "In-Between."

The Bible could be described as a collection of promises. About one-third of the Bible is prophecy; with eighty percent of it having been already fulfilled.[5] What are all of these promises,

---

4   "The Hollow Men" is found in T. S. Eliot's Poems, 1909–1925 (Faber & Faber Limited, 1925)

5   https://www.answerthebible.com/how-much-of-the-bible-is-prophecy/ (Some would argue that the entire Bible is prophecy because it is God's Word. These figures are specific to "predictive prophecy.") https://evidenceforchristianity.org/

stories, poems, and letters all about? They speak to the relationship of God and His creation seen in the arc of redemption from Genesis to Revelation, through God and for His glory.

So, where are we currently within this story arc? In this metanarrative, we reside in the In-Between—between the "already" and the "not yet." Between the eighty percent of fulfilled prophecies and the remaining twenty percent.

A theological term we may apply to this is *prophetic foreshortening*. For believers, we. . .

- Are being purified, yet are already pure (1 John 3:3);
- Know that sin and death are already defeated, yet await their final demise (Romans 5:12–21; Hebrews 2:14);
- Are already redeemed (justification), yet long for final redemption (glorification) (Romans 8:18–30);
- Have been adopted, yet groan for adoption (Romans 8:23);
- Have witnessed the arrival of the Messiah, yet await His return (1 Corinthians 1:8; 2 Timothy 4:8).

To "perceive" that we are in the In-Between is to have eternal perspective.

May we begin to see God all around us in every moment—to see the "bigness" of God in even the smallest things. May we also view people from an eternal perspective. As C.S. Lewis once remarked, "You have never talked to a mere mortal."[6] All people are wonderfully and fearfully crafted in the *Imago Dei*. May we become more aware of God in creation, especially in our fellow man.

> To see a World in a Grain of Sand
> And a Heaven in a Wild Flower,
> Hold Infinity in the palm of your hand
> And Eternity in an hour.
> (William Blake)

---

fulfilled-prophecy-evidence-for-the-reliability-of-the-bible-by-hugh-ross-ph-d/
6   C. S. Lewis, *The Weight of Glory* (Reprint, HarperOne, 2001), 45-46

Attention

In the "modern" world, it seems our attention spans are growing shorter and shorter. Not only do our attention spans lack focus, but what we pay attention to is rather depressing.

Of course, we do not require modern technology and a barrage of digital advertising and entertainment to induce a lack of attention. We are quite capable of it with assistance from only our own myopic self-centeredness. In our stubborn states of distraction and selfishness, we consistently fail to notice beauty in our surroundings. How often do we simply not pay attention?

When was the last time you (not proverbially, but actually) stopped and smelled some roses? Or gazed at the stars on a clear night? Or lost track of time while relaxing and gazing into a campfire or fireplace?

God knows our attention is quick to be distracted and our hearts prone to wander. He knows we need constant reminders (more on this in Chapter 10) and—if we are able to truly pay attention—we will see them all around us.

Through the prophet Hosea, God declares His people are destroyed for a lack of knowledge (Hosea 4:6). I pray these pages meld revived attention with biblical knowledge that gives way to a sort of "visual exegesis."

I first heard this term through artist and pastor Christopher Powers.[7] He takes a passage of Scripture, or simply a verse, and creates art that visually expounds upon the rich meanings of the text. My hope is that we would perform a similar "visual exegesis" process in our day-to-day surroundings; that a mind-renewing experience would take place every time we see one of these reminders; and that we would spontaneously exegete—or draw out—these threads of truth and beauty.

My hope is this book gives readers a new set of lenses through which to see the world around them—to perceive the divine that is all around them—and that once seen, it cannot become unseen. Catch glimpses with me through the veil that hangs between our present state and the kingdom arriving in glory.

---

7   Christopher Powers is the superlatively talented gentleman that created the cover art for this book. To view more of his work visit: fullofeyes.com.

Awe

Finally, the ultimate aim of this book—if there is only one goal it accomplishes—is that it will increase our level of awe of God.

Oh, that we would both redirect misplaced awe and experience heightened capacity for properly placed awe. Paul David Tripp says that almost all of our problems stem from "awe wrongedness," a term he describes as "the war that rages in all our hearts" which is "a war between the awe of God and the awe of self."[8]

There is nothing wrong with being in awe of art, creation, or even people (I am constantly in awe of my wife) but, rather, that all would point us back to the Creator—and that our minds would move with an ever-quickening pace to that destination of beholding our awesome God.

As we move from simple awareness to raptured attention, may we land at a disposition of utter awe—awe of His beautiful creation, of His Living Word, and awe of His sovereign, faithful love through which He weaves all things together for our good and His glory.

If your Bible reading has become stale, may this kindle anew your sense of wonder at the Scriptures and eagerness to continue exploring them.

May these adventures through the Word prove to be beautiful. May they grant new perspectives and capture your attention. May rumination on such wondrously woven themes give way to awe. And may awe lead to an instinctive reflex of deep worship and love, where awe blossoms into action, and where you find yourself loving the Lord your God with all your heart, mind, soul, and strength—and, in turn, loving your neighbor.

The bridge to the song *Build My Life* captures the essence of my prayer over these pages:

> *Holy, there is no one like you*
> *There is none besides you*
> *Open up my eyes in wonder*
> *And show me who you are and fill me*
> *With your heart and lead me*
> *In your love to those around me*

---

8 Paul David Tripp, *Awe: Why it Matters for Everything We Think, Say, and Do* (Wheaton, IL: Crossway, 2015), 33.

I

The Thematic Explorations

1

Gardens, Cultivation, & Bearing Fruit

We're called to a very specific kind of work. To make a Garden-like world where image bearers can flourish and thrive, where people can experience and enjoy God's generous love.

John Mark Comer, "Garden City"

Let us pray God that He would root out of our hearts every thing of our own planting, and set out there, with His own hands, the tree of life, bearing all manner of fruits.

Francois Fenelon

Botanical motifs grow all over the pages of Scripture. Trees, gardens, crop fields, vineyards, and fruit are all used to illustrate divine truths. One does not need to live in an agrarian society to appreciate these metaphors. All that is required is looking outside.

Life Is All about Bearing Fruit. . .

The Bible Begins with Work and a Garden.

> In the beginning God created the heavens and the earth.
> (Genesis 1:1)

The very first verse of the Bible[9] establishes, among several other ideas, the concept of work. We observe that God works. In fact, the Hebrew verb in this verse (*bara'* : "to create") never has a human subject—God can do a type of work that no one else can.

> Then God said, "Let the earth produce vegetation: seed-bearing plants and fruit trees on the earth bearing fruit with seed in it according to their kinds." And it was so. (Genesis 1:11)

God simply *speaks* and brings about complex forms of matter from utter nothingness—*ex nihilo*. He speaks light, water, earth, vegetation, stars, the moon, and every living creature into being. God's work is magnificent, and He declares it good.

There is an important takeaway in these first few verses of the Bible: that work is *good*.

Many people see work as something they begrudgingly do from 9am to 5pm Monday through Friday to make a living and then try to enjoy the other 128 hours left in a week. Work does not always have an esteemed reputation in modern society. We even constantly seek out ways to make work easier on ourselves or work more efficiently so we don't have to spend so much time

---

9   This, by the way, in Hebrew is seven words—more on that in Chapter 8.

on it. We must come to understand that work is an inherently good thing and that we were created to work.

Called to Cultivate

> God blessed them, and God said to them, "Be fruitful, multiply, fill the earth, and subdue it. Rule the fish of the sea, the birds of the sky, and every creature that crawls on the earth."
> (Genesis 1:28)

> The LORD God took the man and placed him in the Garden of Eden to work it and watch over it.
> (Genesis 2:15)

God did not just drop Adam and Eve down in the middle of the woods. No, He took the raw materials He had already made and creatively curated a luscious space. The Master Gardener gifted them a garden.

The very first tasks mankind is assigned can be summed up in one word: fruitfulness. Mankind is given authority and responsibility over all the living creatures, told to fill the earth with creativity and culture, and instructed to fruitfully multiply. It is a call to cultivate in all the facets of life.

Cultivating a garden requires labor. Interestingly, we describe a woman as going into labor when she is about to give birth. Labor yields fruit. Sadly, our cultivation mandate—indeed, all of creation—became subjected to the curse.

Bearing Fruit Becomes Painful

> He said to the woman:
> I will intensify your labor pains;
> you will bear children in anguish.
> Your desire will be for your husband,
> yet he will rule over you.
> And He said to Adam, "Because you listened to your wife's voice and ate from the tree about which I commanded

you 'Do not eat from it':
The ground is cursed because of you.
You will eat from it by means of painful labor
all the days of your life.
It will produce thorns and thistles for you,
and you will eat the plants of the field.
You will eat bread by the sweat of your brow
until you return to the ground,
since you were taken from it.
For you are dust,
and you will return to dust."
Adam named his wife Eve because she was the mother of
all the living. The LORD God made clothing out of skins
for Adam and his wife, and He clothed them.
(Genesis 3:16–21)

The Fall

Here we see the devastating results of disobeying God. Sin is brought into the world and it affects everything—nature, mankind, and our work. All forms of bearing fruit—including bearing children and working for food—now require painful labor. "Work, even when it bears fruit, is always painful, often miscarries, and sometimes kills us."[10]

In the wake of their disobedience, it is comforting to see how God still cares for Adam and Eve even after He has announced their fallen fate. God *works* and produces clothing for Adam and Eve, sacrificing part of His own creation in the process. Even though we are sinful and broken, God still cares and provides for us. He still desires a relationship with us and is willing to sacrifice for it.

Cultivation of our Life Gardens

Gardens need constant care and tending if they are to be beautiful and fruitful. Important areas of life follow this same guideline: The more you put into something, the more you'll get out

---

10   Timothy Keller, *Every Good Endeavor: Connecting Your Work to God's Work* (New York, NY: Penguin, 2012), 89.

of it. This is a rule as natural as gravity. "The person who sows sparingly will also reap sparingly, and the person who sows generously will also reap generously" (2 Corinthians 9:6). Anything worth anything takes discipline.

This may seem simple (and, in many ways, it is), but it is not easy. "For whatever a man sows he will also reap" (Galatians 6:7). Can one sow lack of time and communication with a loved one and expect intimacy? Or sow sugar and slothfulness and expect a fit and healthy body? If we are not happy with the fruit in a realm of life, we should look to change what we are sowing.

Relationships of all sorts require discipline to maintain and, especially, to deepen. In order to have healthy and meaningful relationships, one must work at—or cultivate—them. Let's briefly look at some Life Gardens and what wisdom the Bible has to share.

In the Workplace

> For we are His creation, created in Christ Jesus for good works, which God prepared ahead of time so that we should walk in them.
> (Ephesians 2:10)

What better place to think about our call to cultivation than where we work. This is the place where we are able to reflect Christ through contributing to the welfare of individuals and all of society. Our workplace has the most direct metaphorical correlation with the Garden of Eden.[11]

We are created in the image of God, the *imago dei*, and the desire to cultivate stems from imitating our Abba, our Creator. We worked in Eden and we will work again in the New Heavens and Earth. In the In-Between, however, we must endure the thorns and thistles of the curse. But endure, we will!

> For Christianity is a fighting religion. It thinks God made the world. . . But it also thinks that a great many things

---

11   Much, much more can be said about a biblical perspective on work. A few of my favorite resources from recent years are: *Every Good Endeavor* by Tim Keller; *Culture Making* by Andy Crouch; and *The Sacredness of Secular Work* by Jordan Raynor.

have gone wrong with the world that God made and that God insists, and insists very loudly, on our putting them right again.[12]

When we do good work, we are fighting to make things "on earth as it is in heaven" (Matthew 6:10). When we do good work, working from our souls, "as something done for the Lord and not for men" (Colossians 3:23) then God smiles and the world wonders. By His grace, we will walk in all the good works prepared before us until we walk into eternity where there are no labor pains.

> May our Lord Jesus Christ Himself and God our Father, who has loved us and given us eternal encouragement and good hope by grace, encourage your hearts and strengthen you in every good work and word.
> (2 Thessalonians 2:16–17)

With our Spouse

M: Like a lily among thorns,
so is my darling among the young women.

W: Like an apricot tree among the trees of the forest,
so is my love among the young men.
(Song of Songs 2:2–3)

The relationship between husband and wife is a clear example of a garden that will thrive with consistent care and attention. Like a garden, fruitfulness in marriage requires patience, protection, and proactive work.

Chapter 13 of 1 Corinthians is considered the "love chapter" of the Bible. What is the first adjective Paul uses to describe love? Patience. Whether one has a green thumb or not, it is common sense that plants require patience. So it is when two broken sinners seek to grow in oneness—it takes nurturing, loving patience.

---

12   C.S. Lewis *Mere Christianity* in *The Complete C. S. Lewis Signature Classics* (New York: Harper Collins, 2002), 41.

Protection from subversive outsiders is also critical for fruitfulness. "Catch the foxes for us—the little foxes that ruin the vineyards—for our vineyards are in bloom" (Song of Songs 2:15). A marriage should be protected against anything that could weasel its way into interfering with relational growth.

Yes, all of this takes work. But it is a beautiful "labor of love" that is well worth it. Imitate Christ and the church, grow in oneness, and enjoy the fruit of your marriage vineyard. "Drink, be intoxicated with love!" (Song of Songs 5:1).

With our Children

How happy is everyone who fears the LORD,
who walks in His ways!
You will surely eat
what your hands have worked for.
You will be happy,
and it will go well for you.
Your wife will be like a fruitful vine
within your house,
your sons, like young olive trees
around your table.
In this very way
the man who fears the LORD
will be blessed.
(Psalm 128:1–4)

A family unit—the building block of any society—also needs to be "cultivated" to function properly. Any parent will be quick to tell you—this work brings much "sweat on the brow." Yet, this work is noble and rewarding.

Parents are to instruct children in the way they should go (Proverbs 22:6). Here again, agricultural metaphors can be helpful. As we raise arrows to be sent out (Psalm 127:4), parents must be careful not to not "over water" trying to force growth. Nor should they stand over them, watching and waiting for them to grow and thereby get in the way of the Light that brings true growth.

Notice what the psalmist says leads to a fruitful family: fearing the Lord. It is the beginning of wisdom and the foundation of a blessed family.

With Friends

But the wisdom from above is first pure, then peace-loving, gentle, compliant, full of mercy and good fruits, without favoritism and hypocrisy. And the fruit of righteousness is sown in peace by those who cultivate peace. (James 3:17–18)

Jesus says that He is the vine and we are the branches—He does not say, "and you (singular) are the branch." Believers are not meant to walk through this life alone. We are to sharpen and encourage one another.

As Christians interact, we are to speak to one another in "psalms, hymns, and spiritual songs," always giving thanks to God for everything, and submitting to one another "in the fear of Christ" (Ephesians 5:19–21). Later, in talking about His vine-and-branches metaphor, Jesus tells His disciples: "This is My command: Love one another as I have loved you. No one has greater love than this, that someone would lay down his life for his friends" (John 15:12–13).

With God

How happy is the man
who does not follow the advice of the wicked
or take the path of sinners
or join a group of mockers!
Instead, his delight is in the LORD's instruction,
and he meditates on it day and night.
He is like a tree planted beside streams of water
that bears its fruit in season
and whose leaf does not wither.
Whatever he does prospers.
(Psalm 1:1–3)

We come to the final and most important garden example—our relationship with God.

If we want all of our gardens to be fruitful, we must focus on the source of our nourishment, our living water (more on this in Chapter 5). If we ourselves want to be fruitful and thrive, we must be sustained by God.

Trees do not grow if they are only watered once. Likewise, we must have the discipline to be in constant communion with God through prayer and Scripture reading. We are to take God's instruction and soak it in—to make it a part of our very being. Without this, we cannot expect ourselves—or any of the gardens in our life—to experience growth and fruitfulness. Thankfully, we have the Holy Spirit who guides us.

Fruit borne through the Spirit working in us, which affects all those around us, is *the fruit of the Spirit*:

> But the fruit of the Spirit is love, joy, peace, patience, kindness, goodness, faith, gentleness, self-control. Against such things there is no law.
> (Galatians 5:22–23)

As we Christians faithfully cultivate ourselves to become more Christlike, the Spirit will bear fruit in us (more on this *abiding* later in this chapter). Again, agricultural analogies are being used to describe a spiritual process. These fruitful character traits are what Christians should exemplify as they go out to cultivate various "gardens" and engage this lost world.

Garden Time

In Scripture, gardens consistently show up as places of rest, refocusing, and, yes. . . even romance.

The Garden of Eden was an extraordinary oasis designed by God for Adam and Eve to live abundant lives in communion with God and one another. It was also the setting for the first wedding. Eden echoed with the sound of the first romantic poem as God presented Eve to Adam (Genesis 2:23). Solomon's sultry poem, Song of Songs, contains more garden, fruit, and agricultural references per page than any other book in the Bible. Gardens are an oasis to cultivate relationships.

When Jesus needed to escape and focus solely on communication with the Father, He would escape to the wilderness ("deserted place") or to places such as the Garden of Gethsemane. Perhaps the most overlooked and underestimated spiritual discipline, quiet solitude, is critical for spiritual, physical, and mental health.

To be quiet—to cease striving and know that He is God (Psalm 46:10)—is to hush our physical and spiritual environments. Solitude, as pastor and writer John Mark Comer puts it, "is when you set aside time to feed and water and nourish your soul."[13]

Jesus "often withdrew to deserted places and prayed" (Luke 5:16). In fact, the busier His schedule, the more He practiced this discipline. If Jesus needed this refocusing and rejuvenating quiet solitude, why would we think we do not?

I like to call this spiritual discipline *Garden Time*. It is important we find a "garden" where we can escape life's busyness—a place where we can escape from the things of this world and refocus on the Lord who is able to provide rest and rejuvenation. Garden Time—here's a stillness where you can hear the footsteps of God (like in Eden) and follow Him. However we set up our Garden Time, it has one sole (or perhaps "soul") purpose: to abide.[14]

Eternal Fruit

Abiding Fruit

There is such a thing as bad fruit.

> Beware of false prophets who come to you in sheep's clothing but inwardly are ravaging wolves. You'll recognize them by their fruit. Are grapes gathered from thorn-

---

13   John Mark Comer, *The Ruthless Elimination of Hurry* (Colorado Springs: Waterbrook, 2019), 134.

14   A note on spiritual disciplines, in general: In addition to quiet solitude, examples include: reading and memorizing Scripture, meditation, giving, fasting, and Sabbath-ing (I would suggest prayer is more abiding than it is a discipline. It should envelope any of the disciplines.) As a trellis is to a grapevine, so spiritual disciplines are to the life of believers. These are not checklists; they are structures—the trellises—that help us abide and, hence, bear fruit.

> bushes or figs from thistles? In the same way, every good
> tree produces good fruit, but a bad tree produces bad
> fruit. . . . So you'll recognize them by their fruit.
> (Matthew 7:15–20)

Just as actions are louder than words, so people's fruit is a result of their true intentions. Faith without works is dead (James 2). Faith is a renewed lens through which we see the world in a different light, and that perspective will affect our every action. Therefore, an active faith should be a fruitful faith. Now, we are not the ones to judge the hearts of others; however, we should be aware that we can recognize false teachers and believers by their fruit. Does the fruit in our own lives have integrity?

So, how do believers produce this "good fruit" that Jesus speaks of? The answer is one word which is at the nucleus of the Christian life: Abide.

> I am the vine; you are the branches. The one who remains
> in Me and I in him produces much fruit, because you can
> do nothing without Me. . . . My Father is glorified by this:
> that you produce much fruit and prove to be My disciples.
> (John 15:5, 8)

Abiding is faith. Abiding is loving God with all your heart, soul, mind, and strength. Abiding is steadfast cultivation of an ever-growing relationship with Jesus. Good fruit is simply the beautiful by-product of abiding that brings nourishment to your soul and the souls of those around you.

Connection to Jesus does not mean, however, that life will always be smooth sailing.

Uncomfortable Grapevines

On a vacation to Napa Valley, I was able to tour a gorgeous vineyard. During the tour, the guide said something that immediately caught my attention: "You don't want comfortable grapevines."

The guide went on to explain that their vineyard focused on the quality, not quantity, of grapes. In order to produce such excellent grapes, the vineyard keepers "stressed" the grapes in several ways. They kept the topsoil to a minimum depth and regularly pruned the vines to focus on smaller, quality clusters of grapes. He also explained how the California weather was perfect for the vines. It would get very hot during the day and "stress" the vines but then it would always be cool at night to let the vines recover. All of this led to fewer grapes with thicker skins with excellent flavor and qualities for fine wine making.

Like the vines in Napa, we are more fruitful when pruned—and we should expect to be pruned. Jesus tells us that the Father prunes every branch that produces fruit so that it will produce more (John 15:2). Pruning, of course, is not easy and painless. "No discipline seems enjoyable at the time, but painful. Later on, however, it yields the fruit of peace and righteousness to those who have been trained by it" (Hebrews 12:11). Through the iron-sharpening of fellow believers, natural consequences of our choices, or the sharp Word that surgically cuts to the marrow and brings conviction, God prunes our character to look more and more like Jesus. He cuts away bad habits, false beliefs, and sin that so easily entangles so that we may fruitfully flourish.

Let us strive to accept it with joy and thanksgiving because God is helping us. The Father disciplines those He loves (Hebrews 12:5–13). Godly discipline calls for rejoicing for it verifies connection to the True Vine.

Harvest

When we are connected to the True Vine, a kind of fruit that should result is new disciples (Matthew 28:18–20; 2 Timothy 2:2). To become "fishers of men" is to plant and water with the gospel so that there might be a harvest of souls. Indeed, with compassion for the crowds, Jesus told His disciples, "The harvest is abundant, but the workers are few. Therefore, pray to the Lord of the harvest to send out workers into His harvest" (Matthew 9:37–38).

The lives of the Israelites, with their feasts and holidays, very much revolved around agricultural cycles throughout the year. The related language of firstfruits, harvest, and gleanings is metaphorically important in the prophets and the New Testament.[15]

Jesus did not always give explanations for His parables. However, He did interpret the parable of the Wheat and the Weeds to the disciples:

> He replied: "The One who sows the good seed is the Son of Man; the field is the world; and the good seed—these are the sons of the kingdom. The weeds are the sons of the evil one, and the enemy who sowed them is the Devil. The harvest is the end of the age, and the harvesters are angels." (Matthew 13:37–39).

Again, we find that the harvest is related to the saving of souls. And Jesus is the firstfruits of the harvest! As Paul explains, "If the firstfruits offered up are holy, so is the whole batch. And if the root is holy, so are the branches" (Romans 11:16). And since believers "have the Spirit as the firstfruits" we are rooted in Christ. He is the True Vine and "the firstfruits of those who have fallen asleep" (Romans 8:23; 1 Corinthians 15:20).

So, disciples of Jesus are co-laborers with one another and with Christ (Philippians 4:3; 1 Corinthians 3:9; 3 John 8). By grace, may we view the people around us as more than "mere mortals" and faithfully work towards an abundant harvest.

God, the Good Gardener

In all of our Life Gardens, we can pull weeds, scatter seed, plant, or water but, ultimately, God gives the growth.

He is the One who planted a good work in us and will cultivate it unto completion (Philippians 1:6). As we labor, it is His strength that works powerfully in and through us (Colossians 1:29). He is the One who equips us "with all that is good to do His will, working in us what is pleasing in His sight, through Jesus Christ. Glory belongs to Him forever and ever" (Hebrews 13:21). All we must do is abide in, and trust, our good Gardener.

---

15 An entire book could delve into this symbolism. The phases of the harvests also appear to correlate to the different resurrections of the righteous: Christ as firstfruits; the Church age as the main harvest; Tribulation and Old Testament saints as the gleanings. This is beyond our scope here, but worthy of exploration.

Isn't it fitting that Mary mistook the risen Jesus as a gardener (John 20:15)? Mankind brought about damnation in a garden but then Jesus defeated it in a garden (John 19:41). Reading between the lines, I like to think Jesus stepped out of the tomb, took a deep breath of fresh air, and then looked down and saw something in the garden He wanted to set right. And when He returns, all things *will* be set right and we will share in the fruit of eternal life (Romans 6:22).

2

No Shadow of Turning

This light gives a view of those things that are immensely the most exquisitely beautiful, and capable of delighting the eye of the understanding. This spiritual light is the dawning of the light of glory in the heart.

Jonathan Edwards

A glory gilds the sacred page,
Majestic like the sun;
It gives a light to every age;
It gives, but borrows none

William Cowper,
"The Bible, the Light of the World"

ightsaber battles are commonplace in our house. This is not because we have any Jedi Knights or Sith Lords under our roof, but rather three boys (their sister generally avoids such skirmishes). *Star Wars* contains what is certainly one of the most famous fictional uses of light and darkness.

Archetypally, light represents goodness, hope, truth, divinity, and guidance. It is the light side of the force. It is Gandalf the White casting beams of light toward the dark clouds of the enemy and wisely guiding other characters of Tolkien's classics. It is the truth that shines in Plato's allegory of the cave or a divine highlight in an otherwise shadowy Baroque painting.

In recent centuries, physicists have been confronted with the fact that the very nature of light appears to have transcendent attributes. Thanks to work done by brilliant minds like Albert Einstein, we know that at the speed of light, time stops. In light of this property (pun intended), photons (particles of light) are therefore ageless. Light is, in effect, immortal.[16]

Light is one of most common physical attributes to describe God and all things related to the heavenly realm in the Bible. God dwells in "unapproachable light" (1 Timothy 6:16) surrounded by brilliant light "like that of a rainbow in a cloud on a rainy day" (Ezekiel 1:28). At Jesus' transfiguration, His face "shone like the sun" and His clothes became "white as light" (Matthew 17:2). Paul was confronted by "an intense light from heaven" during his famous encounter with Jesus on the road to Damascus (Acts 22:6). The angel sitting on the stone at Jesus' empty tomb had an appearance "like lightning" (Matthew 28:2).[17]

While the above examples fit well with light representing divinity, not surprisingly, these other symbolic meanings of light can also be found in Scripture.

The Lord is our guidance. He says, "Along unfamiliar paths I

---

16   There is a fabulous chapter in Dr. Richard Swinson's book, *More than Meets the Eye*, for more on the detailed science of light and how it relates to God.

17   This divine light may also be referred to as the *Shekinah glory* (or simply, Shekinah or Shechinah). It comes from a root word that means "to dwell" or "to Tabernacle." Often, in the Bible it is referred to as "the glory of the Lord." This special physical manifestation of God appears throughout Scripture. Typically, it is in the form of light but often accompanied by clouds, fire, and thick darkness. Dr. Arnold Fruchtenbaum does an excellent job tracking the location of the Shekinah through the Bible in Appendix IV of his book *The Footsteps of the Messiah*.

will guide them; I will turn the darkness into light before them and make the rough places smooth" (Isaiah 42:16). His Word is a lamp for our feet and lights our path (Psalm 119:115). He is the lamp that turns our darkness into light (2 Samuel 22:29). It is His wisdom that is light while our folly is darkness (Ecclesiastes 2:13).

The Lord is our hope. For how else can we say, "The LORD is my *light* and my salvation—whom shall I fear?" (Psalm 27:1). It is by our hope in Him that, though we go through dark times, we can say, "the LORD will be my light" and "He will bring me out into the light; I will see His righteousness" (Micah 7:8–9).

The Lord is truth. Indeed, "The LORD's lamp sheds light on a person's life, searching the innermost parts" (Proverbs 20:27). Nothing is hidden from the light of truth and no darkness can remain secret; for even darkness is not dark to Him (Daniel 2:22, Psalm 139:11–12). This light penetrates mind, body, and spirit.

It seems almost in our nature to associate light with good and darkness with evil. We intuitively assign the meanings that light should be symbolic for goodness, divinity, guidance, hope, and truth. Let us delve deeper into this biblical motif that appears woven into humanity's design.

Reflection

While not the first sentence of the Bible, it may be one of the most famous: "And God said, 'Let there be light,' and there was light" (Genesis 1:3). On the first day of creation, God speaks light into being. One could argue He speaks time itself into being, as now "night" and "day" are established and set into motion and we then have the very first day.

One of the most critical properties of light is that it can be reflected. It is to this characteristic that we owe our sense of sight. Unless an object itself emits light, the only way we humble humans can view it is via the light the object reflects.

Creation is one beautiful reflection of the Creator. As the sun shines and opens our eyes to the natural beauty around us, so the universe shows us the majesty of the One who is "sustaining all things by His powerful word" (Hebrews 1:3). The visible reflects the invisible. Yes, "His eternal power and divine nature have been clearly seen since the creation of the world, being understood through what He has made" and it leaves mankind without excuse for not "seeing" God (Romans 1:20). Nowhere is this more evident in creation than with mankind.

Imago Dei

So God created man in His own image;
He created him in the image of God;
He created them male and female.
(Genesis 1:26–27)

In the "image" of God; that is how you and I were created. An image may be defined as: "An optically formed duplicate, counterpart, or other representative reproduction of an object, especially an optical reproduction formed by a *lens* or *mirror*."[18] It is a *reflection*.

This is what sets us apart from the rest of creation. We are handcrafted and breathed to life by God Himself; living reflections of our Creator; imbued with innate worth and purpose. Even with our diversity within humanity—male, female, ethnicity, language—there is something special about all that reflects our one, glorious Father. And, one day, it will be beautiful to behold "a vast multitude from every nation, tribe, people, and language, which no one could number, standing before the throne and before the Lamb" reflecting His glory back to Him in praise and worship (Revelation 7:9). For this is why we were created.

It is His light that illuminates who we are. Much like the sun, moon, and other heavenly lights, this divine light also nourishes, guides, and wows us.

Pro-vision

It is amazing to see the significance light plays in the physical realities around us and even inside of us. We need light, of course, even to observe these phenomena. The tilt of the earth and its distance from the sun are perfectly set for us to be warmed but neither fro-

---

18   American Heritage Dictionary, 5th ed, emphasis added.

zen nor incinerated. This warmth keeps animals and humans alive while also influencing ocean currents, the water cycle, the turning of seasons, and other crucial patterns of nature. Photosynthesis provides oxygen but also food for man and beast. Sunlight nourishes our bodies in regard to vitamin D, hormone and nitric oxide production, and regulating our circadian rhythms. Whether we realize it or not, we are desperately dependent on light.

Not only does light nourish us and our world, but it itself is beautiful. The majestic glow of a sunrise signaling mercies anew (Lamentations 2:22–23); colors bursting forth in the evening sunset; the scintillating stars against a black canvas, giving precise navigational aid and with a vastness numbered only by the Lord (Psalm 147:4)—beauty and awe.

Despite our modern technologies, ninety-five percent of this vastness remains a mystery to use. Influenced by NASA, we have simply coined it "dark matter" and "dark energy." My mind goes to God questioning Job from the whirlwind:

> Have you ever in your life commanded the morning
> or assigned the dawn its place. . .
> Have you seen the gates of deep darkness?
> . . .Where is the road to the home of light?
> Do you know where darkness lives,
> so you can lead it back to its border?
> Are you familiar with the paths to its home?
> . . . What road leads to the place where light is dispersed?
> (Job 38:12, 17b, 19, 20, 24a)

It is the Lord God who creates, sustains, and bends all light to do His will. (Here's a quick tip: if God ever asks a question, it isn't because He does not know the answer!) He is the One who "wraps himself in light as with a garment" and "stretches out the heavens like a tent" (Psalm 104:2).

The heavenly lights speak to God's majesty and might but also His common grace. When we feel the warmth of the morning sun on our faces, we should be reminded that "He causes the sun to rise on the evil and the good" (Matthew 5:45)—His common grace reflected in the cycles of nature.

Hallelujah!
Praise the Lord from the heavens;
praise Him in the heights.
Praise Him, all His angels;
praise Him, all His hosts.
Praise Him, sun and moon;
praise Him, all you shining stars.
Praise Him, highest heavens,
and you waters above the heavens.
Let them praise the name of Yahweh,
for He commanded, and they were created.
He set them in position forever and ever;
He gave an order that will never pass away.
(Psalm 148:1–6)

Refraction

We should be in awe of creation, but not mistake it for the Creator. How quick we are as humans to turn good things into God things. God knows this and warns in Deuteronomy:

When you look to the heavens and see the sun, moon, and stars—all the array of heaven—do not be led astray to bow down and worship them. The Lord your God has provided them for all people everywhere under heaven. (Deuteronomy 4:19)

While we were created as reflections and for reflection, we live in a sinful and fallen world. There is a schism between the image bearer and the One we are to image.

At the risk of offending my more scientifically minded audience, I am going to use some principles regarding light in physics to help us further explore the symbolism of light in the Bible.

When light strikes a flat plane, the law of reflection states that reflection is at an angle equal to that of the original wave of light. The "angle of incidence" is, in theory, perfectly equal to the "angle of reflection."

Due to the reality of physics, there is no such thing as perfect

100 percent reflection in the natural world. When light strikes an object, some part of it is absorbed, refracted, or otherwise does not reflect.

Refraction is when light moves between two mediums of varying density and the waves change direction. This is why a pencil placed in a glass half-filled with water will appear to bend.

The pencil appears to have changed, but its structure is the same. It is the refracted light that alters the perception of the pencil. It is a shift in perspective.

It is our premise that these many created phenomena have rich spiritual and scriptural parallels. This side of eternity, we can only see "indistinctly" or "indirectly" as looking "in a mirror" (1 Corinthians 13:12). Mirrors in ancient times were not as clear as modern-day mirrors; however, I think the metaphor still holds. Though we are called to be "salt and light" none of us is able to perfectly reflect God's love and light. Even though we are being sanctified, our sinful nature keeps us from fully seeing and reflecting as we should.

This fallenness in our natures and the world can also twist our perspective on what is real and true. This "spiritual refraction" is most prevalent during dark and difficult times. We can lose sight of God's illuminating truth when we are living in sin, impacted by the sinful actions of others, or suffering the effects of a fractured world—such as sickness or natural disaster. We are tempted to believe the distorted lies of the enemy who accuses us and questions God's character. It is a battle of perspective. The truth remains unchanged. We must not let shifting circumstances bend our view of the True Light.

Such storms in this life are inescapable. But God's promises cannot be washed away. Did you know that refraction is also responsible for rainbows? This is the promise the Lord made with Noah along with all creation. God told Noah that:

> This is the sign of the covenant I am making between Me and you and every living creature with you, a covenant for all future generations. . .the bow will be in the clouds, and I will look at it and remember the everlasting covenant between God and all the living creatures on earth. (Genesis 9:12, 16)

This is a promise from the One who keeps *all* of His promises.

The prophet Ezekiel wrote of his heavenly visions in this way: "like that of a rainbow in a cloud on a rainy day. This was the appearance of the form of the LORD's glory" (Ezekiel 1:28).[19] His promises are always present and He grants us signs to remember them. Even when we are caught up in the dark storms of life, our perspective does not change His promises. He redeems our spiritual refraction into rainbows.

Exposure

Scripture frequently speaks of darkness in both a physical and spiritual sense. As we shall continue to see, the physical and spiritual meanings are often intertwined.

The ninth plague that came upon Egypt, as pharaoh hard-heartedly continued to refuse to release God's people, was darkness:

> Then the LORD said to Moses, "Stretch out your hand toward heaven, and there will be darkness over the land of Egypt, a darkness that can be felt." So Moses stretched out his hand toward heaven, and there was thick darkness throughout the land of Egypt for three days. One person could not see another, and for three days they did not move from where they were. Yet all the Israelites had light where they lived.
> (Exodus 10:21–23)

There was utter darkness; no sense of direction; no distinction between night and day; a black blanket so oppressing that the Egyptians didn't move about. Imagine fumbling around trying to find the bathroom during those three days!

In the New Testament, there is also a moment we see physical darkness fall upon the land. As Jesus hung on the cross, "from noon until three in the afternoon darkness came over the whole land" (Matthew 27:45; see also Mark 15:33, Luke 23:44). The light

---

19   All of electromagnetic radiation is technically light, but the human eye can only see a small section of wavelengths (other examples are: Gamma rays, X rays, UV light, infrared, microwaves, and radio waves). So, a rainbow displays the full spectrum of visible light. We have a God who wants to make Himself visible to us!

in the land darkened as the Light of the world was dying. The "sun's light failed" as the Son of God appeared to many to have failed (Luke 23:45). The "Lamb of God who takes away the sins of the world" was slain at the same hour the evening Passover sacrifice was taking place in the temple (John 1:29).[20]

With both the ninth plague and the sacrifice of Jesus, the supernatural physical darkness clearly coincides with a deep spiritual darkness.

This spiritual darkness is where we all dwell without God's saving light, for we are "people walking in darkness" and "living in a land of darkness" (Isaiah 9:2)—lost; blind; enclosed in the gloom of a spiritual grave; dead in our "trespasses and sins" (Ephesians 2:1), not only without light, but resenting the light. For "everyone who does evil hates the light, and will not come into the light for fear that their deeds will be exposed" (John 3:20). All iniquities and secret sins are laid bare in the light of God's presence (Psalm 90:8). The darkness wants nothing to do with the light.

The darkness, however, cannot overcome the light (John 1:5). We who have been saved have seen the light and are now "children of light" (Ephesians 5:8). Jesus, the ultimate light, has illuminated the path of salvation.

> Don't participate in the fruitless works of darkness, but instead expose them. For it is shameful even to mention what is done by them in secret. Everything exposed by the light is made clear, for what makes everything clear is light. Therefore it is said:
> Get up, sleeper, and rise up from the dead,
> and the Messiah will shine on you.
> (Ephesians 5:11–14)

---

20   Due to the patterns of our moon and sun, scientists are able to calculate precise historical celestial happenings. A partial eclipse lasting about three hours occurred on April 3rd, AD 33. It so happens that day was also a Friday (the day before the Sabbath). See https://eclipse.gsfc.nasa.gov/LEhistory/LEhistory.html#ref.

No Shadow of Turning

Here's an interesting experiment: Take a lit candle and set it near a blank wall. Next, take a flashlight and shine it onto the candle, casting a shadow onto the wall. What do you see? The shadow on the wall is that of the candle and the wick—but the flame has no shadow.

God is the greatest light. He is the "Father of lights" and "with Him there is no variation or shadow cast by turning" (James 1:17). There is no darkness whatsoever in Him. He is wholly good and "is not tempted by evil, and He Himself doesn't tempt anyone" (James 1:13). His light is unchangeable and unmatched in brilliance, purity, and goodness.

This great light pierced the darkness when Jesus came and dwelt among us.

> In the beginning was the Word, and the Word was with God, and the Word was God. He was with God in the beginning. Through him all things were made; without him nothing was made that has been made. In him was life, and that life was the light of all mankind. The light shines in the darkness, and the darkness has not overcome it.
> There was a man sent from God whose name was John. He came as a witness to testify concerning that light, so that through him all might believe. He himself was not the light; he came only as a witness to the light.
> The true light that gives light to everyone was coming into the world.
> (John 1:1–9)

Jesus is the true light. He is a "light for revelation to the Gentiles and glory to [God's] people Israel" (Luke 2:32). He brings light and is light itself, for He says, "I am the light of the world. Whoever follows me will never walk in darkness, but will have the light of life" (John 8:12). He illuminates our path to salvation and He *is* the path to salvation.

Jesus is the only true reflection of God we have humanly seen, for He is "the image of the invisible God" (Colossians 1:15). Jesus

Himself told His disciples, "If you know Me, you will also know My Father. From now on you do know Him and have seen Him" (John 14:7). The Father of lights truly does give every perfect gift—and none so perfect as giving us Himself.

Christ is the perfect image, and His followers are to *image* Him. To be a Christian means you have seen "the light of the gospel that displays the glory of Christ, who is the image of God" (2 Corinthians 4:4). Those who have been called "out of darkness into His marvelous light" are to to be "conformed to the image" of Christ (1 Peter 2:9, Romans 8:29). How are we to do this?

The Word (Jesus) and the Word (the Bible) guide us in becoming more Christlike. To reflect, we must first bask in His light. Then we are able to walk in the light and, in turn, be lights to a dark and dying world.

Bask and Walk

I would submit that to bask in the light of Christ is to be in *awe* of Him; to be awestruck as if taking in the most glorious sunrise ever seen; an awe that reflexively gives way to worship; that drives us to walk and talk and think in a worshipful way. Paul writes to the church in Corinth, "For God, who said, 'Let light shine out of darkness,' made his light shine in our hearts to give us the light of the knowledge of God's glory displayed in the face of Christ" (2 Corinthians 4:6). May our hearts bask in the glory of His light.

Notice also that this light brings knowledge. This knowledge is found through Spirit-infused consumption of Scripture. We must know the "sacred Scriptures, which are able to give you wisdom for salvation through faith in Christ Jesus" (2 Timothy 3:15). How else are we supposed to know how to walk in the light if we do not internalize and practice what this "lamp unto our feet" instructs?

This knowledge leads to action. Notice it is described as walking—this is a journey, not a light switch. This is the process we call *sanctification*. We must cast off the old and "put on the new self" while "being renewed in knowledge according to the *image* of [our] Creator (Colossians 3:10). This takes practice and steadfastness.

> Now this is the message we have heard from Him and de-
> clare to you: God is light, and there is absolutely no dark-
> ness in Him. If we say, "We have fellowship with Him,"
> yet we walk in darkness, we are lying and are not practic-
> ing the truth. But if we walk in the light as He Himself is
> in the light, we have fellowship with one another, and the
> blood of Jesus His Son cleanses us from all sin.
> (1 John 1:5–7)

To walk in the light is to practice the truth. For what good is the light unto our path if we always stay put? Truth must rewire both our minds and deeds. And we do not accomplish this alone. Fellowship with other believers in the body of Christ—the church—is another essential ingredient.

As one of my pastors used to repeat, "There are no 'Lone Ranger' Christians." We were made for fellowship. The church is compared to a body where every part is essential to its healthy functioning (Ephesians 4). How are we supposed to be giving with no one to receive? How are we to practice the truth in love if not in community with other saints?

To love one another is to remain in the light (1 John 2:8–10). To refer back to 1 Peter 2, the church is the "chosen race, a royal priesthood, a holy nation, a people for His possession, so that you may proclaim the praises of the One who called you out of darkness into His marvelous light" (v. 9). We can help one another walk in the light. This may involve lovingly exposing the areas of darkness in each other's lives. It may be shedding light on the spiritual gifts you see in your fellow brothers and sisters in Christ. It certainly involves leading, teaching, exhorting, discipling, and encouraging one another as we are all seeking to reflect Jesus and be conformed into His image.

This individual and collective sanctification is a beautiful transformation. Putting on a new lens—an eternal perspective—a consistent beholding that leads to becoming.

> We all, with unveiled faces, are looking as in a mirror
> at the glory of the Lord and are being transformed into
> the same image from glory to glory; this is from the

> Lord who is the Spirit.
> (2 Corinthians 3:18)

This is a Spirit-led, progressively glorious transformation as we—by grace—have unveiled spiritual eyes to look into the divine light.

Perhaps no theologian has referenced the symbol of light as much as Jonathan Edwards. In his sermon, *A Divine and Supernatural Light*, he writes in reference to this verse from 2 Corinthians:

> This light is such as effectually influences the inclination, and changes the nature of the soul. It assimilates the nature to the divine nature, and changes the soul into an image of the same glory that is beheld.

This transcendent light affects everything it touches. Only it can change our "inclinations" for "it is God who is working in you, enabling you both to *desire* and to *work out* His good purpose" (Philippians 2:13). Our nature is so marred by sin we are not even inclined to righteousness. But when the supernatural light of Christ shines upon us, it completely changes our desires, our abilities, our very souls.

Though this transformation will not be completed this side of eternity, may it be a glorious journey of ever-deeper abiding with the True Light.

Not Just Receivers, but Reflectors

We bask in the Divine Light, we walk in the light. We follow Christ—the light of the world—and the Scriptures—which illuminate our path. We are being sanctified and exhorting brothers and sisters in Christ to do the same. But we are not to keep this glorious light contained within ourselves and the church.

> You are the light of the world. A town built on a hill cannot be hidden. Neither do people light a lamp and put it under a bowl. Instead they put it on its stand, and it gives light to everyone in the house. In the same way, let your light shine before others, that they may see your good

deeds and glorify your Father in heaven.
(Matthew 5:14–16)

Let us not hide our light, for we did not receive the good news to be selfish with such a gift. We are to bring the light to our neighbors. The term *good deeds*, of course, includes one of the main actions Jesus instructs us to do: fulfill the Great Commission. Once we have received the light, we become lights and we are to share it unto the ends of the earth. Charles Spurgeon puts it this way: "The Bible is not the light of the world, it is the light of the Church. But the world does not read the Bible, the world reads Christians! 'You are the light of the world.'"

It is a sort of "spiritual photosynthesis" where we are nourished and then, in turn, generate natural by-products of loving our neighbors as ourselves. Our deeds do not change people—only the Divine Light can accomplish that. But we should shine brightly, nonetheless, and pray that the Spirit may "unveil" the mind of unbelievers all over the globe. Let us not be just receivers, but also reflectors.

Night Is Nearly Over

Nowhere does the Bible say that walking in light, being conformed to Christ's image, and being salt and light is an easy journey. But this is our calling as Christians, nonetheless. What, then, can help motivate us to persevere? The imminence of eternity.

Paul writes in his letter to the Romans that "now our salvation is nearer than when we first believed" (Romans 13:11). This salvation he refers to is not our initial conversion, but looking forward to ultimate salvation at the end of all things. "The night is nearly over, and the daylight is near, so let us discard the deeds of darkness and put on the armor of light" (v. 12). The darkness of this world will not last forever. A new dawn is coming when all evil shall be extinguished and light and good will prevail. The urgency of eternity should powerfully impact our choices in the present.

For believers, this is a perspective brimming with hopeful expectation. We have been rescued from the "domain of darkness" and transferred into "the kingdom of the Son" and will share in the "inheritance in the light" (Colossians 1:2–13). Our inheritance will last forever (Psalm 37:18). It is "imperishable, uncorrupted, and unfading" (1 Peter 1:4). The Holy Spirit, who helps us walk in the light during this life, is the down payment of this inheritance (Ephesians 1:11–14). The Father of Lights has a good gift waiting for the saints!

In each of these passages, the nearing of a new dawn and the accompanying inheritance are connected with sanctifying work and joyful hope in the present. In Romans 13, Paul connects our coming day of salvation to an instruction to "walk with decency, as in the daylight" (v. 13). In the first chapter of Colossians, Paul's prayer connects the inheritance in the light with "endurance and patience, with joy" (v. 11). Peter links it with rejoicing with "inexpressible and glorious joy" even though "now for a short time you have had to struggle in various trials" because we "are receiving the goal of your faith, the salvation of your souls" (1 Peter 1:3–9). How incredible! This news is so amazing that even "angels desire to look into these things" (v. 12).

As a part of this unfading inheritance, believers themselves will undergo a resplendent transformation. The saints "will shine like the sun" in the everlasting kingdom (Matthew 13:43). We shall receive a perfected heavenly body. Jesus "will transform the body of our humble condition into the likeness of His glorious body, by the power that enables Him to subject everything to Himself" (Philippians 3:21). What exactly these redeemed bodies will look like, we do not fully know. However, the brief descriptions from Paul relate to our theme of light.

> There are heavenly bodies and earthly bodies, but the splendor of the heavenly bodies is different from that of the earthly ones. There is a splendor of the *sun, another of the moon, and another of the stars*; for one star differs from another star in splendor. So it is with the resurrection of the dead:
>
> Sown in corruption, raised in incorruption;
> sown in dishonor, raised in glory;

sown in weakness, raised in power;
sown a natural body, raised a spiritual body.

If there is a natural body, there is also a spiritual body.
And just as we have borne
the *image* of the man made of dust,
we will also bear
the *image* of the heavenly man.

Brothers, I tell you this: Flesh and blood cannot inherit the kingdom of God, and corruption cannot inherit incorruption.
(1 Corinthians 15:40–44)

Our heavenly bodies will be pure, incorruptible, and immortal so that we may fully receive our inheritance in the light (see the whole of 1 Corinthians 15). This image that was "indistinct" and unattainable while in our natural bodies becomes crystal clear, and we are transformed by Christ to finally image Him as we should. And what image of Jesus do we see at this time? In the first chapter of Revelation, "He had seven stars in His right hand; a sharp double-edged sword came from His mouth, and His face was shining like the sun at midday" (v. 16). It is the same promise that Jesus made in Matthew 13: we will shine like the sun.

Keep fighting the good fight.
Keep running the race.
The night is nearly over.
A glorious new dawn is on the horizon.

3

Come to the Water

Come, thou Fount of every blessing;
tune my heart to sing thy grace;
streams of mercy, never ceasing,
call for songs of loudest praise

Robert Robinson, 1758 AD

God is in the rain

Alan Moore, V for Vendetta

Water is powerful.

Water is essential to life as we know it. More than half of the earth's surface—and our own bodies—is made up of water. It has the unique ability to naturally exist in all three physical states: solid, liquid, and gas. This characteristic is foundational to the hydrologic cycle of condensation and evaporation that most natural systems and organisms in our world rely on.

With water being so essential to the natural world, it is no wonder that one of its primary archetypal meanings is life. It can represent nourishment, new life, or rebirth. Another universal meaning is renewal or cleansing. Lastly, it may represent time-lessness or eternity.

We find similar meanings throughout the Bible as it pertains to both the literal and spiritually metaphorical references to water.

Lifespring

Who cuts a channel for the flooding rain
or clears the way for lightning,
to bring rain on an uninhabited land,
on a desert with no human life,
to satisfy the parched wasteland
and cause the grass to sprout?
Does the rain have a father?
Who fathered the drops of dew?
Whose womb did the ice come from?
Who gave birth to the frost of heaven
when water becomes as hard as stone,
and the surface of the watery depths is frozen?
(Job 38:25–30)

Common grace is theological talk for the graciousness God shows to all of humanity. The Presbyterian theologian, John Murray, defined common grace as "every favor of whatever kind or degree, falling short of salvation, which this undeserving and sin-cursed world enjoys at the hand of God."[21] It is the gift of ev-

---

21   John Murray, "Common Grace," in *Collected Writings of John Murray*, vol. 2 (Edinburgh, UK: Banner of Truth, 1977), 96.

ery breath—of every moment. It can be seen in any restraining of evil that we are blissfully unaware of, or any good thing that we currently enjoy. The very ability to read or listen to this book is grace. And it can be seen in the rain. For God "sends rain on the righteous and the unrighteous" (Matthew 5:45). Barnabas and Pual informed the belligerent crowds in Lystra of this concept, explaining:

> In past generations He allowed all the nations to go their own way, although He did not leave Himself without a witness, since He did what is good by giving you rain from heaven and fruitful seasons and satisfying your hearts with food and happiness.
> (Acts 14:16–17)

As God's rhetorical questions to Job illustrate, God owns, sustains, and is in charge of all waters. How amazing that He actively showers the earth and humanity with common grace!

> Sing to the LORD with thanksgiving;
> play the lyre to our God,
> who covers the sky with clouds,
> prepares rain for the earth,
> and causes grass to grow on the hills.
> (Psalm 147:7–8; see also all of Psalm 104 in regard to God's sovereign common grace.)

Rains, rivers, and springs are, of course, physical symbols of nourishment. The locations of successful civilizations were often determined by the weather and presence of large bodies of water, as surviving—and thriving—were dependent on agriculture, fishing, and trade. Even in the garden of Eden, there was an unnamed river that watered its flora and from which four rivers originated (Genesis 2:10–14), displaying that all life came out of the garden. The Promised Land is described as a "good land, a land with streams of water, springs, and deep water sources, flowing in both valleys and hills" (Deuteronomy 8:7).

Consistently, these forms of water also show up in the Bible as metaphors for spiritual nourishment. The Lord's appearance and presence are compared to "the spring showers that water the land" (Hosea 6:3). The Lord is our shepherd who leads us beside quiet waters (Psalm 23). As water revitalizes the land and our bodies, so the Lord rejuvenates our souls.

However, as we shall see, not all symbols of water in the Bible are placid and refreshing. . .

Calamity and Cleansing

Deep Waters

While water is vital and nourishing, it can also be frighteningly powerful and even dangerous. Since 1980, the total cost of natural disasters (which are all related to water—or lack thereof, in the case of wildfires and droughts) in the US has exceeded $2.1 trillion (yes, trillion, not billion).[22] In the United States, drowning is the leading cause of death for children ages one to four.[23]

Water can bring life.

Water can bring destruction.

The destructive nature of water can also be found in both physical and metaphorical depictions in Scripture. We all go through storms in life—whether they are the forces of nature, of man, or of a more spiritual nature.

Due to the fallen state of this world, turbulent trials are inevitable. Whether hurricanes or hailstorms, accidents or disease, there is often no individual to blame for our storms. This is the sin-infected world we reside in. The psalmist writes about these treacherous waters:

> Save me, God,
> for the water has risen to my neck.
> I have sunk in deep mud, and there is no footing;
> I have come into deep waters,

22   NOAA National Centers for Environmental Information (NCEI) U.S. Billion-Dollar Weather and Climate Disasters (2024). https://www.ncei.noaa.gov/access/billions/, DOI: 10.25921/stkw-7w73

23   https://ndpa.org/drowning-facts-and-data/

and a flood sweeps over me.
I am weary from my crying;
my throat is parched.
My eyes fail, looking for my God.
(Psalm 69:1–3)

This is what the storms of life feel like. We find ourselves struggling to keep our heads above water, gasping for air, and wondering if the deep waters will swallow us whole. We can feel like the disciples crying out to a sleeping Jesus as they were caught in a violent storm on the sea of Galilee, "Lord, save us! We're going to die!" (Matthew 8:25).

While it may be due to a broken world or the sinful actions of others, oftentimes our storms are caused by our own sin.

Jonah, the obstinate and disobedient prophet, runs in the opposite direction after receiving his assignment from God. He boards a ship that promptly encounters a terrible storm. The crew, at Jonah's request, toss him overboard. The famous great fish (probably a whale, but we do not know for sure), appointed by God, then shows up and swallows him. Inside the belly of the fish, Jonah prays:

I called to the LORD in my distress,
and He answered me.
I cried out for help in the belly of Sheol;
You heard my voice.
You threw me into the depths,
into the heart of the seas,
and the current overcame me.
All Your breakers and Your billows swept over me.
But I said: I have been banished
from Your sight,
yet I will look once more
toward Your holy temple.
The waters engulfed me up to the neck;
the watery depths overcame me;
seaweed was wrapped around my head.
(Jonah 2:2–5)

Jonah's own sin leads him down to the port of Joppa to find a ship, down to the lowest part of the ship, and down into the watery depths (Jonah 1).[24] Sinful decisions can lead to drowning. So often, we stir up our own storms.

Throughout the Old Testament, the spiritual state of Israel is also reflected in symbols connected to water. In instructing His chosen people, God tells them:

> If you carefully obey my commands I am giving you today, to love the LORD your God and worship Him with all your heart and all your soul, I will provide rain for your land in the proper time, the autumn and spring rains (Deuteronomy 11:13–15)

However, if Israel is idolatrous and disobedient, God says:

> Then the LORD's anger will burn against you. He will close the sky, and there will be no rain; the land will not yield its produce, and you will perish quickly from the good land the LORD is giving you.
> (Deuteronomy 11:17)

God always keeps His word. Indeed, we see this pattern play out in stories throughout the rest of the Old Testament. Israel's spiritual droughts correspond with physical droughts.

Geographically, Israel is situated on an arid plateau that is uniquely dependent on rain. Just before the warning given in Deuteronomy 11:17, God tells His people that:

> The land you are entering to possess is not like the land of Egypt, from which you have come, where you sowed your seed and irrigated by hand as in a vegetable garden. But the land you are entering to possess is a land of mountains and valleys, watered by rain from the sky. It is a land the LORD your God cares for. He is always watching over it from the beginning to the end of the year.

---

24 The word "down" is repeatedly used in the beginning of Jonah, reflecting his spiritual state.

(Deuteronomy 11:10–12)

Egypt had the fertile Nile delta which helped provide the abundant sustenance necessary for that area's great ancient civilizations. The largest source of fresh water for Israel is the sea of Galilee.[25] It does not seem surprising that God would select a land for His people where they would be strikingly reliant on the One who provides the rain.

Often, the extent to which Israel was relying on God was reflected in their rainfall. Under king Ahab, who "did more to provoke the LORD God of Israel than all the kings of Israel who were before him," the faithful prophet Elijah prays and shuts the skies for three-and-a-half years (1 Kings 16:33; see also 1 Kings 17–18). When the Israelites pay attention to their own houses but not to rebuilding the temple, God tells them "on your account, the skies have withheld the dew and the land its crops" (Haggai 1:10).

While droughts paralleled the spiritual state of Israel, it was simultaneously a form of judgment. Sometimes that judgment is not in the drying up of water, but in a deluge.

Surely, the most famous example of water in the Bible is the flood and Noah's ark. There are many scholars that believe that, up until this time, there was no rain as "the LORD God had not made it rain on the land. . . . But water would come out of the ground and water the entire surface of the land (Genesis 2:5–6). How amazing that Noah obeyed when he had never witnessed rain.

Of course, faith is "the reality of what is hoped for, the proof of what is not seen" (Hebrews 11:1). And "by faith Noah, after he was warned about what was not yet seen and motivated by godly fear, built an ark to deliver his family" (v. 7). He understood the reality and necessity of righteousness in the face of impending retribution.

God's wrath was not without reason, for He "saw that man's wickedness was widespread on the earth and that every scheme his mind thought of was nothing but evil all the time" and "He was grieved in His heart" (Genesis 6:5–6). Six chapters into the Bible, and humankind has broken God's heart. Even His fury flows from

---

25 https://storymaps.arcgis.com/stories/019ef73c3df0458b87f8600e9ac6c2b2

His love and, indeed, He did pour out His "fury on them like water" (Hosea 5:10). For "all the sources of the watery depths burst open, the floodgates of the sky were opened, and the rain fell on the earth 40 days and 40 nights" (Genesis 7:11–12).[26] Here was divine judgment in the form of deep waters.

Our final example of water used as God's instrument for punishment is also a well-known Old Testament narrative: the parting of the Red Sea.

After Pharaoh releases the Israelites, they are led by God to the shores of the Red Sea. However, they soon find themselves pursued by Pharaoh and his grand army. The Lord instructs Moses to lift up his staff and stretch out his hand over the sea. Then, with a powerful east wind, the Lord divides the waters "and the Israelites went through the sea on dry ground, with the waters like a wall to them on their right and their left" (Exodus 14:21–22). Pharaoh's army pursued but "the LORD threw them into the sea" and none survived (vv. 27–28).[27]

Just as water can both give and take life, so it can be a spiritual blessing or judgment. As Peter writes, "The heavens and the earth were brought about from water and through water by the word of God. Through these waters the world of that time perished when it was flooded" (2 Peter 3:5–6). There was both creation and destruction.

It is noteworthy that in both of these aqueous adjudications, God's mercy is simultaneously on display. He protects His chosen people—the righteous Noah and his family and the Israelites—through the judgments. God does not keep them *from* the waters, but is with them and guides them *through* the waters. Peter makes this connection between the eight people on the ark being "saved through water" and baptism (1 Peter 3:20–21; more on baptism later in the chapter).

While God, in His providential protection, most certainly often keeps us from calamities, His promises are consistently about being with us *through* trials. When we feel the waters rising, God says, "I will be with you when you pass through the waters, and

---

26   There will be more on the significance of the number 40 in Chapter 8.

27   There is great, vivid imagery in the song the Israelites wrote after this event. Also, interestingly, the very next story in Exodus involves water and God's provision.

when you pass through the rivers, they will not overwhelm you" (Isaiah 43:2). When life's problems feel like an impassable sea, it is the Lord "who makes a way in the sea, and a path through surging waters" (43:16). When life feels like a barren wasteland, "the LORD will always lead you, satisfy you in a parched land, and strengthen your bones. You will be like a watered garden and like a spring whose waters never run dry" (Isaiah 58:11).

Storms will come, but the Lord is with us—always!

> The depths of the sea became visible,
> the foundations of the world were exposed,
> at Your rebuke, LORD,
> at the blast of the breath of Your nostrils.

> He reached down from heaven
> and took hold of me;
> He pulled me out of deep waters.
> (Psalm 18:15–16)

Poured Out

Water is invaluable. To the ancient Israelites, water was life. This is why it is important to notice examples in the Bible when it is "wasted."

In 1 Samuel 7, the Israelites gathered at Mizpah and the prophet Samuel judged them for their worshiping of idols. They fasted, confessed their sins, and "they drew water and poured it out in the LORD's presence" (1 Samuel 7:6).

Let's observe another instance of water poured out.

Have you ever been so thirsty that three of your friends made a twenty-five-mile round-trip trek to fetch you a drink? King David was.

While Bethlehem was occupied by a Philistine garrison and David was hiding in a cave, he desired a drink from the well at the gate to Bethlehem. Three of his choice warriors then snuck behind enemy lines and brought the water back to David. Deeply moved by their life-risking gesture, David refused the drink and instead "he poured it out to the LORD" (2 Samuel

23:16; see also 1 Chronicles 11:15–19).[28]

What is the significance of these offerings? In a region where water is so precious, it seems like a terrible waste. It is unrecoverable and seems in some ways to point to death (see how this is referred to in 2 Samuel 14:14). Of course, what is a sacrifice if it doesn't cost something?

The Water & The Blood

In this section, we must take a moment to examine the inextricable connection in Scripture between water and blood (and by proxy, wine). Both represent life and are essential to life. Both show up jointly in famous biblical passages. And both relate profoundly to our motifs of cleansing and being poured out. From the blood of the animal that clothed a fallen Adam and Eve to the blood-dipped robe of the Messiah, an entire book could be written on the blood-themed scarlet cord woven through Scripture. Let us give attention to the highlights of symbolic connections that it shares with water.

Blood is very much like water in that whether it renders life or death is dependent upon context. A healthy heart circulating blood through arteries and veins brings vitality. Remove that same blood, and the result is death.

Illustrating this point, the first plague God brought upon Egypt turned the Nile to blood for seven days, killing the fish and rendering it undrinkable (Exodus 7:14–25). In Revelation, the two witnesses possess the power to turn waters into blood (Revelation 11:6). In those same end days, the second and third bowls of judgment poured out will turn the sea, rivers, and springs to blood (Revelation 16:3–4). The Lord's judgments confront these groups with the reality that the blood of God's people is on their hands. The angel of the waters says: "Because they poured out the blood of the saints and the prophets, You also gave them blood to drink" (Revelation 16:6).

God instructed the Israelites not to "eat the blood, since the blood is the life, and you must not eat the life with the meat" and instead

---

28 While David was likely physically thirsty, his heart thirsted for justice and the end of the Phillistine occupation.

to "pour it on the ground like water" (Deuteronomy 12:23–24). The blood of sacrifices and offerings was to be poured out at the base of the altar (see Leviticus 4). "According to the law almost everything is purified with blood, and without the shedding of blood there is no forgiveness" (Hebrews 9:22). Therefore, it was set apart.

So, we discover that blood and water are both related to cleansing and life.

Blood and water from Jesus' eyes and face poured onto the ground at Gethsemane. When the Roman soldiers pierced Jesus' side, confirming His death, what gushed forth? Blood and water (John 19:34).[29] What two sacraments does the church practice? Baptism and the Lord's Supper. "For there are three that testify: the Spirit, the water, and the blood—and these three are in agreement" (1 John 5:7–8). Jesus is our drink offering, poured out for our forgiveness (Luke 22:20). Through the calamity of the cross, we are cleansed.

> O precious is the flow
> that makes me white as snow;
> no other fount I know;
> nothing but the blood of Jesus.

Washing

Ritual washings are an important part of many cultures, and this was especially true for the Hebrews. For the priests to fail to wash with water before entering the tent of meeting or even approaching the altar was to risk death (Exodus 30:19–20). Washing clothes and/or bathing in water was prescribed in many of the Old Testament laws. These washings were the difference between being unclean—and restricted from fellowship with God and kin—or clean, and therefore accepted back into the normal routines of worship and community.

---

29 Typically, those executed via crucifixion died of exposure, exhaustion, and asphyxiation. This process could be lengthy (hence, the soldiers broke the legs of the men on the left and right to speed up the process). Water coming from Jesus' side would indicate pericardial fluid had built up. This is generally related to a heart attack or similar heart episode. No one took Jesus' life from Him; He laid it down (John 10:18). Love is laying down one's life for others (John 15:13). I would submit that it was not any person or process that killed Jesus. His earthly body died from a broken heart.

While modern readers would see obvious sanitary reasons for many of these laws—such as bathing after touching an animal carcass—there were spiritual dimensions as well. Washings and sprinklings of water marked both purification and inaugural religious events. Purification water was sprinkled on people or places for them to be declared clean (Numbers 8:7; 31:23).

Water, of course, cannot actually purify our souls. Spiritual cleansing requires something more than what is skin deep. Even if we "wash with lye and use a great amount of soap" the stains of our sins remain (Jeremiah 2:22). We need God to "create a clean heart" within us (Psalm 51:10). All of these ritual washings and sprinklings pointed to the One who would wash away our sins. The greatest symbol saturated with these truths is baptism.

Baptism is a communal celebration of God's work in us. It is "an outward and visible sign of an inward and invisible grace."[30] Baptism is the beautiful first act of obedience for the Christian where we identify with Jesus in His baptism, obedience, death, burial, and resurrection. It is an outward work displaying living faith in our living Lord and Savior. Together, with the church, it is a sacred celebration. Passing through the waters, we declare that Jesus has brought us out of slavery into service to Him, out of wandering into the promised land, out of death and into abundant life.

The Word and Water (Drink Up!)

The average human can only go about 100 hours without water.[31] A loss of more than ten percent of body weight due to dehydration is a medical emergency.[32] As remarkably resilient as the human body is, without water we wither away at a frightening pace.

Water's life-preserving and nourishing qualities are reflected in many metaphors in God's Word relating to, well, God's Word.

---

30   This quote is from St. Augustine. See: https://rcdow.org.uk/att/files/faith/catechesis/baptism/sacraments.pdf

31   https://www.nbcnews.com/health/health-news/pulled-rubble-after-16-days-water-secret-survival-f1C9876099

32   https://www.encyclopedia.com/medicine/diseases-and-conditions/pathology/dehydration.

> Pay attention, heavens, and I will speak;
> listen, earth, to the words of my mouth.
> Let my teaching fall like rain
> and my word settle like dew,
> like gentle rain on new grass
> and showers on tender plants.
> For I will proclaim Yahweh's name.
> Declare the greatness of our God!
> (Deuteronomy 32:1–3)

This passage is from the beginning of the Song of Moses. That same day, Moses went up to Mount Nebo—as the Lord instructed—and died while looking off in the distance to Canaan, the Promised Land. After reciting his song to Joshua and the Israelites, Moses instructed them:

> Take to heart all these words I am giving as a warning to you today, so that you may command your children to carefully follow all the words of this law. For *they are not meaningless words to you but they are your life*, and by them you will live long in the land you are crossing the Jordan to possess.
> (Deuteronomy 32:46–47)

Surely Moses told the Israelites to listen countless times. However, even his own carelessness (an instance related to water) prevented him from stepping foot in the Promised Land. The instructions are the same to us today. We must heed God's words. Pay attention! For only when we listen do we experience peace "like a river" and "righteousness like the waves of the sea" (Isaiah 48:18). The words of the Lord bring life. Pay attention to them.

God's word is living and effective (Hebrews 4:12). Not one word is devoid of meaning. All His words are powerful and vitalizing.

> For just as rain and snow fall from heaven
> and do not return there
> without saturating the earth
> and making it germinate and sprout,

and providing seed to sow
and food to eat,
so My word that comes from My mouth
will not return to Me empty,
but it will accomplish what I please
and will prosper in what I send it to do.
(Isaiah 55:10–11)

Our words are rarely as graceful as falling snow and they often fail in our intentions. We fail to give proper advice, to deliver needed encouragement, or to persuade when it counts. Often, in our sinfulness, we simply put our foot in our mouth.

But, as reliable as the water cycle functioning, so is the reliability of God's words. As the famous nineteenth-century British preacher Charles Spurgeon comments:

> Go, find ye the snowflakes winging their way like white doves back to heaven! Go, find the drops of rain rising upward like diamonds flung up from the hand of a mighty man to find a lodging-place in the cloud from which they fell! Until the snow and the rain return to heaven, and mock the ground which they promised to bless, the word of God shall never return to him void.[33]

Indeed, even if a day came where raindrops reversed their course, God's word is true and dependable. For though heaven and earth will pass away, His words never will (Matthew 24:35).

And the Lord's words raining down naturally produce fruitfulness. This is the true response to these true words: "Ground that has drunk the rain that has often fallen on it and that produces vegetation useful to those it is cultivated for receives a blessing from God" (Hebrews 6:7). Thorns and thistles are not the result of soaking up His words, but rather blessing—blessing to the one who listens and to others nearby.

How happy is the man

---

33 From his sermon "Pleading Prayer" June 23, 1887, Scripture: Psalms 119:49, From: *Metropolitan Tabernacle Pulpit* Volume 33.

who does not follow the advice of the wicked
or take the path of sinners
or join a group of mockers!
Instead, his delight is in the LORD's instruction,
and he meditates on it day and night.
He is like a tree planted beside streams of water
that bears its fruit in season
and whose leaf does not wither.
Whatever he does prospers.
(Psalm 1:1–3)

The man who trusts in the LORD,
whose confidence indeed is the LORD, is blessed.
He will be like a tree planted by water:
it sends its roots out toward a stream,
it doesn't fear when heat comes,
and its foliage remains green.
It will not worry in a year of drought
or cease producing fruit.
(Jeremiah 17:7–8)

This fruitfulness stemming from drinking of the endless reservoirs of God's word is a perpetual fruitfulness. There is no anxiety over external influences, but rather delight and trust in the Lord's instruction and faithfulness.

May we always beware of dehydrating our spirits. May His words continually saturate and nourish our minds and souls. May we be trees planted by streams of the water that is God's Word.

Living Water

Then the One seated on the throne said, "Look! I am making everything new." He also said, "Write, because these words are faithful and true." And He said to me, "It is done! I am the Alpha and the Omega, the Beginning and the End. I will give water as a gift to the thirsty from the spring of life.
(Revelation 21:5–6)

We have looked at how the God-designed natural qualities of water beautifully connect with truths throughout the Bible—how it is life-giving and life-sustaining, its ability to cleanse, and water's displays of sheer power. These scriptural metaphors continue in relation to humanity's most dire need: salvation.

Her name is not mentioned in the Bible, but she asked Jesus a crucial question: "So where do You get this 'living water'?" (John 4:11). This is from the famous exchange between Jesus and the Samaritan woman at Jacob's well.[34] Jesus answers her:

> Everyone who drinks from this water will get thirsty again. But whoever drinks from the water that I will give him will never get thirsty again—ever! In fact, the water I will give him will become a well of water springing up within him for eternal life.
> (John 4:13–14)

This is the living water; the powerful water that washes away sin; the water that brings the soul to life and nourishes it forevermore.

Internal springs of water reflect the wonderful mystery of salvation that is Christ in us (Colossians 1:27). Later in John's Gospel, Jesus is teaching at the temple on the final day of the Feast of Tabernacles and proclaims:

> If anyone is thirsty, he should come to Me and drink! The one who believes in Me, as the Scripture has said, will have streams of living water flow from deep within him.
> (John 7:37–38)

John then writes that Jesus "said this about the Spirit" because "those who believed in Jesus were going to receive the Spirit." He then explains that the "Spirit had not yet been received because Jesus had not yet been glorified" (v. 39).

How marvelous! This good news is that we can receive the gift

---

34   Verse four states that Jesus "had to" go through Samaria. Although this was the most efficient route, most Jews took the long way around to avoid Samaria. Clearly, Jesus had greater plans.

of the living water and have the same power that raised Christ from the dead —the Holy Spirit—flowing within us (Romans 8:11)! And through the Spirit, to *"overflow"* with hope, comfort, righteousness, gratitude, and love (Romans 15:13; 2 Corinthians 1:5; 2 Corinthians 3:9; Colossians 2:7; 1 Thessalonians 3:12, respectively).

Amazingly, the entire Trinity shows up in living water symbolism. Jesus is the vessel through whom we obtain the Spirit welling up inside of us and who grants us access to the fountain from whom the living water pours forth—the Father (Jeremiah 2:13, 17:13). Hallelujah! The Lord is our salvation!

For believers, there is an aspect of prophetic foreshortening where living water is our current—but also future—reality. Streams of living water—the Holy Spirit—flow within us now; however, there are future visions of living water to eagerly anticipate.

Both Ezekiel and Zechariah speak of a future of water that "comes from the sanctuary" that is, Jerusalem (Ezekiel 47:12; see also Zechariah 14:8). This living water flows "in summer and winter alike" and " On that day Yahweh will become King over all the earth—Yahweh alone, and His name alone" (Zechariah 14:8–9). Where this water travels "leaves will not wither" and "fruit will not fail" and "there will be life everywhere the river goes" (Ezekiel 47:9, 12). This future reality is where our faith is made sight— where we arrive at the fountain of living water.

> They will no longer hunger;
> they will no longer thirst;
> the sun will no longer strike them,
> nor will any heat.
> For the Lamb who is at the center of the throne
> will shepherd them;
> He will guide them to springs of living waters,
> and God will wipe away every tear from their eyes.
> (Revelation 7:16–17)

Is your soul parched?
Come to the water.

Is your sin a crimson stain?
Come to the water.

Do you desire to have life, and have it more abundantly?
For your cup to overflow?
Come to the water.

Have you been chasing mirage after mirage?
Come to the water.

Do you wish to nourish your mind and spirit?
Come to the water.

Do you thirst for a reality where God will wipe away every tear and
death, grief, and pain are no longer. . .?
Come to the water.

4

Hearts Ablaze

The only hope, or else despair
Lies in the choice of pyre or pyre—
To be redeemed from fire by fire.

T. S. Eliot, Four Quartets 4: Little Gidding

Oh take your flame, ignite the world
Under the name above all names,
we declare that the glorious One lives
Take your flame, ignite the world

For Today, Seraphim

In an archetypal sense, fire commonly represents transformation, renewal, purification, passion, divine power, and emotion.

In English, we use phrases such as *hotheaded, fired up, fight fire with fire,* and *fire in one's belly.* All of these idioms express strong emotions and drive.

Appearing Aflame

When God decides to manifest Himself in the Bible, He often appears in the form of fire.[35]

Moses had a front-row seat to these holy and miraculous blazes. Firstly, there was his encounter with God through the burning bush. The Lord's purity and power are on display as He instructs Moses to not step any closer and to remove the sandals from his feet, saying the place where Moses is standing is holy ground (Exodus 3:5).

As Moses continues to fulfill his calling received at the burning bush to lead the Israelites, God shows up again to guide them as a pillar of cloud by day and of fire by night which "never left its place in front of the people" (Exodus 13:21–22).

Three months after exiting Egypt, the Israelites make camp at the base of mount Sinai. Moses brings the people "out of the camp to meet God" and "Mount Sinai was completely enveloped in smoke because the Lord came down on it in fire. Its smoke went up like the smoke of a furnace, and the whole mountain shook violently" (Exodus 19:17–18). Again, God's fiery presence makes the mountain holy so that the Israelites have to consecrate themselves for three days and may not cross a boundary onto the mountain lest they perish.

Moses goes up on the mountain and receives instruction and the Ten Commandments inscribed on stone tablets by the "finger of God" (Exodus 31:18),[36] during which time the incredible inferno continues:

---

35 See the footnote about the "Shekinah glory" for more about God's intentional, glorious manifestations.

36 How amazing is that!? I wonder what God's handwriting looks like. . .

> The glory of the LORD settled on Mount Sinai, and the
> cloud covered it for six days. On the seventh day He
> called to Moses from the cloud. The appearance of the
> LORD's glory to the Israelites was like a *consuming fire* on
> the mountaintop. Moses entered the cloud as he went up
> the mountain, and he remained on the mountain 40 days
> and 40 nights.
> (Exodus 24:16–18)[37]

What amazing displays of glory and power Moses was allowed
to witness!

There is one more famous Old Testament character we shall
look at in relation to God's presence in the form of fire: Elijah.

In one of the most well-known (and rather humorous) ac-
counts in the Old Testament, the prophet Elijah singly challenges
450 prophets of Baal to a grand contest to determine who really
is the One Living God. The challenge? Each team gets some wood
and a bull to sacrifice. Both are to call out to their God, and the
God who answers with fire is the true God.

The prophets of Baal go first, driving themselves into a cul-
tish frenzy. Meanwhile, Elijah watches on and mocks them:
"Perhaps Baal is taking a potty break!" (That's my paraphrase of
what the Hebrew implies.) Of course, nothing happens on the
altar to Baal.

Next, Elijah has four pots of water poured on the altar three
times so that it is drenched and the water even fills a trench he
had dug around the altar.[38] Even then, Elijah had faith that the
rains would return (and they did, as recorded several verses later). He prays to the Lord to show that He is God and to turn the
wayward hearts of Israel back. Then:

> Yahweh's fire fell and consumed the burnt offering, the
> wood, the stones, and the dust, and it licked up the wa-
> ter that was in the trench. When all the people saw it,

---

37   See Chapter 8 for more on the numbers 7 and 40.
38   Israel was in a time of disobedience towards the Lord and therefore experi-
encing a drought, which makes pouring water on the altar even more significant
(see previous chapter for more on "wasted" water). Consider how close the Medi-
terranean sea is to Mount Carmel; it is not impossible that salty water was used.

they fell facedown and said, "Yahweh, He is God! Yahweh, He is God!"
(1 Kings 18:38–39)

Such heat that even the twelve stones Elijah had arranged were disintegrated! This was not the last time Elijah saw God's presence in the form of fire.

Elijah is one of only two men (that we know of) who were taken up by God before dying a natural death—the other being Enoch (see Genesis 5:24). And he went out in style! As Elijah and Elisha were walking and talking "a chariot of fire with horses of fire suddenly appeared and separated the two of them. Then Elijah went up into heaven in the whirlwind" (2 Kings 2:11). Imagine arriving at the gates of heaven with that ride!

Not only does the presence of God on earth involve fire, but heavenly visions do as well. Daniel has a dreaming vision and sees the Ancient of Days and says "His throne was flaming fire; its wheels were blazing fire" and that "a river of fire was flowing, coming out from His presence" (Daniel 7:9–10).

In Ezekiel's heavenly vision, he sees at first "great cloud with fire flashing back and forth and brilliant light all around" and with his vision of God he witnesses:

a form with the appearance of a human on the throne high above. From what seemed to be His waist up, I saw a gleam like amber, with what looked like fire enclosing it all around. From what seemed to be His waist down, I also saw what looked like fire.
(Ezekiel 1:27)

Ezekiel also catches a glimpse of the seraphim (literally, "the burning ones") whose appearance "was like the appearance of burning coals of fire and torches" (Ezekiel 1:13). These are the perpetually combustible angels that call out "Holy, holy, holy is the LORD of Hosts" (Isaiah 6:3). We see again fire representing holiness and divine power, as well as an agent of purification when the seraphim touch Isaiah's lips with a burning coal (Isaiah 6; more on this purifying quality later).

God's red-hot manifestations are not limited to the Old Testament.

Jesus Himself said, "I came to bring fire on the earth, and how I wish it were already set ablaze!" (Luke 12:49). What is this fire? I agree with MacLaren's exposition that is the life-giving gospel mission of Jesus and that "if we catch the celestial fire, we shall flash and blaze, but the fire which we catch is not originated on earth. In a word it is God's Divine Spirit which Christ came to communicate to the world".[39]

The Feast of Weeks, or Pentecost, is celebrated seven weeks (or fifty days; hence, the Greek root *pente*) after Passover. This feast celebrated God's blessing in the firstfruits of the wheat harvest (Leviticus 23:16). It also commemorates the giving of the law on Mount Sinai covered earlier. Notice that seven week period lines up with the third month after the Israelites left Egypt (see Exodus 19).

It is no coincidence that the God who makes "winds His messengers, flames of fire His servants" determined to pour out the Spirit on this day (Psalm 104:4). The apostles were gathered together on Pentecost when

> Suddenly a sound like that of a violent rushing wind came from heaven, and it filled the whole house where they were staying. And tongues, like flames of fire that were divided, appeared to them and rested on each one of them. Then they were all filled with the Holy Spirit and began to speak in different languages, as the Spirit gave them ability for speech.
> (Acts 2:2–4)

What an outpouring of blessing from the Lord! Peter quotes the prophet Joel and the fulfillment of the promise that God would pour out His Spirit on all humanity. This baptism of fire and the Holy Spirit[40] led to an abundant harvest of firstfruits. That same day, about 3,000 people believed and were baptized.

Unbelievable blessing, a substantial harvest, and new covenant

---

39   MacLaren, A. "Fire on Earth (Luke 11:49) by Alexander MacLaren." Blue Letter Bible. Last Modified 17 Feb 2022. https://www.blueletterbible.org/comm/maclaren_alexander/expositions-of-holy-scripture/luke/fire-on-earth.cfm
40   This is a reference to John the Baptist's prophecy, see Matthew 3:11; Luke 3:16.

fulfillment—no longer was the law written on stone tablets but the law was now written on the hearts and minds of believers (Hebrews 10:15–16; Jeremiah 31:33–34). Pentecost and pyrotechnics—it was the perfect day for the church to be born.

Disciples of Jesus all have the flame of the Spirit inside of them. Whereas the prophets of old had special anointing and revelation, now believers everywhere should resonate to the marrow of our being with Jeremiah: "His message becomes a fire burning in my heart, shut up in my bones" (Jeremiah 20:9). We possess unparalleled access to the Living Word *and* we have the Holy Spirit dwelling within. Paul exhorts Timothy to "keep ablaze the gift of God that is in you" (2 Timothy 1:6). What a beautiful and gracious gift it is!

May our burning desire be to have His praise on our lips and to see the gospel spread like wildfire! As we grow in our walk with the Lord, may we, like the disciples who encountered the risen Jesus on the road to Emmaus, say, "Weren't our hearts ablaze within us while He was talking with us on the road and explaining the Scriptures to us?" (Luke 24:32). Is not your heart ablaze with awe of God?

Wrath Kindled

Courtesy of often overzealous street corner preachers, fire and brimstone are among the first images people think of in relation to God. Of course, this is most definitely a one-dimensional view of God; however, when He does pour out His wrath, it is fiery and ferocious.

First, we must briefly examine the nature of God's wrath, lest we constrain it to meager human lenses. Contrary to what unhinged street preachers would have us think (and, to be honest, sometimes how we feel about ourselves), God is not up in heaven with a lightning bolt eagerly waiting to smite an unsuspecting sinner.

God is love (1 John 4:8) and therefore all of His attributes are bound up with His love—including anger and wrath. Not only are these linked to love, but—if we may say so—they do not seem to be His first instinct.

Right in the middle of the symmetrical structure of the book of Lamentations is the statement, "He does not enjoy bringing affliction or suffering on mankind" (Lamentations 3:33).[41] God does not revel in the punishment of mankind. He does not want any to perish but rather to repent (2 Peter 3:9). I am reminded of when Abraham negotiated with God about relenting from destroying Sodom and Gomorrah if only a handful of righteous people could be found in the cities (Genesis 18:16–33). Or when Moses interceded on behalf of the Israelites on Mount Sinai when God mentions allowing His anger to "burn against" the people and destroying them so He could start over with Moses (Exodus 32:7–14). God does exact judgment, but there is something about Him that perpetually leans toward mercy.

Pastor Dane Ortlund in his superb book, *Gentle and Lowly*, describes it this way:

> Unlike us, who are often emotional dams ready to break, God can put up with a lot. This is why the Old Testament speaks of God being "provoked to anger" by his people dozens of times (especially in Deuteronomy; 1–2 Kings; and Jeremiah). But not once are we told that God is "provoked to love" or "provoked to mercy." His anger requires provocation; his mercy is pent up, ready to gush forth.[42]

While our natural reaction to being wronged by another is vengeance, God's (super)natural reaction is grace and mercy.

So, we see that "kindled" is a fitting term—God's anger must be kindled, but never His grace. Though the Lord is *slow* to anger, He is not *never* to anger. When the Lord's kindled anger ignites to wrath—beware. His blazing vengeance is unmatched.

> Look, they are like stubble; fire burns them up. They cannot deliver themselves from the power of the flame. This is not a coal for warming themselves, or a fire to sit beside!
> (Isaiah 47:14)

---

41   Lamentations contains remarkable artistry in prose and structure. Chiasm and alphabetic acrostics can be found. It is an oft-neglected book that is fascinating to study.

42   Dane Ortlund, *Gentle and Lowly: The Heart of Christ for Sinners and Sufferers* (Wheaton, IL: Crossway, 2020), 148.

There are myriad of examples in the Bible of fire symbolism to describe God's rage. The prophets, especially, contain many of these images.

Isaiah writes, "Look, Yahweh comes from far away, His anger burning and heavy with smoke. His lips are full of fury, and His tongue is like a consuming fire" (Isaiah 30:27). Micah describes the effect of this heat: "The mountains will melt beneath Him, and the valleys will split apart, like wax near a fire" (Micah 1:3). Ezekiel uses the image of a smelting furnace: "Yes, I will gather you together and blow on you with the fire of My fury, and you will be melted within the city" (Ezekiel 22:20–21).

"Who can withstand His indignation? Who can endure His burning anger? His wrath is poured out like fire, even rocks are shattered before Him" (Nahum 1:6). The answer to Nahum's rhetorical questions is, of course: No one.

God's fury is not contained to imagery and metaphors. Several times in Scripture we see very real fire rage from the heavens.

The Israelites experienced this firsthand. They began complaining about hardship in the wilderness and God's "anger burned, and fire from the LORD blazed among them and consumed the outskirts of the camp" (Numbers 11:1). Only when Moses prayed did the fire cease. The Israelites had a pattern of naming locations after events, and this place was given the name Taberah—which means blaze. Something to think about the next time we catch ourselves complaining. . .

And then there are the cities that have become synonymous with fire and brimstone—Sodom and Gomorrah. From Abraham's negotiation with the Lord, we know that not even ten righteous people resided there. Due to their extreme wickedness, "the LORD rained burning sulfur on Sodom and Gomorrah" and in the aftermath "smoke was going up from the land like the smoke of a furnace" (Genesis 19:24, 28). Dust and ashes.

The consummate and most terrible form of fiery wrath is a place of unquenchable fire—of ceaseless burning. It is a place of darkness, weeping, and gnashing of teeth (Matthew 22:13).[43] It is "the lake that burns with fire and sulfur" (Revelation 21:8). This

---

43   It is interesting to note there is fire, yet no light. To experience all of the burning qualities and yet none of the positive qualities of fire is, frankly, terrifying.

is Gehenna—the Lake of Fire.

It is not the aim of this writing to wrestle with reconciling God's judgment and wrath with His equally excellent qualities of mercy and love. On such matters, the only comment will be that He is God and we are not. The point is that this "blazing furnace" as Jesus called it in His warnings, is the frighteningly real example of God's ultimate wrath (Matthew 13:42, 50).

Instead of singing praises, there is gnashing of teeth. Instead of God Himself wiping away every tear, there is perpetual weeping. Instead of a place where "moth and rust do not destroy" it is a place where "the worm does not die" (Mathew 6:19–20; Isaiah 66:24; Mark 9:44, 46, 48). In many ways, hell is as difficult to imagine as heaven. How is it that the hellfire never runs out of fuel? How do the flames lick but never fully consume?

I would submit it is the opposite of all that heaven is and has. There is no fruitfulness. There is no light of life. There is no living water. It is the utter absence of God. As immeasurably great is the Lord's eternal love in heaven, so there is commensurate wrath in the lake of fire.

Conflagration

Before the Israelites cross over the Jordan into the Promised Land, Moses warns them numerous times about idolatry. He instructs them:

> Be careful not to forget the covenant of the LORD your God that He made with you, and make an idol for yourselves in the shape of anything He has forbidden you. For the LORD your God is a *consuming fire*, a jealous God. (Deuteronomy 4:23–24)

Moses also reminds Israel that the Lord "let you hear His voice from heaven to instruct you. He showed you His great fire on earth, and you heard His words from the fire" (Deuteronomy 4:36). In his exhortations, Moses makes several references to the fact that they "did not see any form on the day the LORD spoke to you out of the fire at Horeb" (Deuteronomy 4:12, 15).

They are not to mistake created, physical things for the one true invisible Creator. The Lord our God is a jealous God.

What does it mean that God is jealous? Is He insecure? Does He wrongfully desire something? He cannot tolerate sin, so it cannot be covetousness—which would go against the tenth commandment. God does not envy anyone's house or good looks as we fallen humans do. Nothing can compare to Him and He created and owns everything—so God has nothing to envy anyway. No, this jealousy—this consuming fire—is about His burning passion for our good and His glory.

We will see that this jealousy is intimately intertwined with the other facets of fire symbolism—holiness, wrath, and refinement. The Lord is uncompromising with His holiness, jealous even in His judgment, and produces golden results through His refining fire.

Unceasing Sacrifice

Burnt offerings were one of the main prescriptions for the Israelites to show honor and glory to the Lord. The Lord Himself sent down fire to consume the inaugural sacrifices for both the start of the priests' ministry and the dedication of Solomon's temple (Leviticus 9:24; 2 Chronicles 7:1). God also commanded Aaron and his sons that the "fire must be kept burning on the altar continually; it must not go out" (Leviticus 6:12–13). The meticulous instructions for the various sacrifices and offerings were to be fearfully followed; otherwise, it could bring the Lord's jealous judgment.

When two of Aaron's sons brought unauthorized fire offerings before the Lord, it did not go well. As they they presented their incense "fire came from the LORD and burned them to death before the LORD" (Leviticus 10:2). In what seems like a less-than-comforting response, Moses tell Aaron that "this is what the LORD meant when He said:

> I will show My holiness
> to those who are near Me,
> and I will reveal My glory
> before all the people."
> (Leviticus 10:3)

God's instructions have a purpose and they are to be taken seriously. It is not wise to be haphazard regarding His holiness. Nothing sinful or unclean can come near the consuming fire without being incinerated. We would do well to serve God "acceptably, with reverence and awe, for our God is a consuming fire" (Hebrews 12:28–29).

But God is not merely concerned with order and regulations; He is jealous for our hearts.

Eyes for you

The sixteenth-century theologian, John Calvin, famously remarked that "the human heart is a perpetual idol factory." We can be quick to judge the Israelites, yet our hearts are no less fickle. We envy, grumble, and seem to constantly look for idols (including ourselves) rather than God. How often do we sacrifice time, money, and talent to these false gods? We incite God's burning jealousy with our idol manufacturing.

The Lord is rightfully due all honor, praise, and glory. But He wants more than ritualistic sacrifices. He wants our whole being—heart, mind, soul, and strength (Matthew 22:36–37). "The sacrifice pleasing to God is a broken spirit" (Psalm 51:17). "To obey is better than sacrifice, to pay attention is better than the fat of rams" (1 Samuel 15:22). He desires loyalty, seeking after knowledge of Him, and mercy rather than burnt offerings (Hosea 6:6; Matthew 9:13). To love the Lord and, in turn, "to love your neighbor as yourself, is far more important than all the burnt offerings and sacrifices" (Mark 12:33).

Did you know this? Have you pondered this?
The Lord of the universe wants you!
He is jealous for you.

Often in Scripture, God uses the metaphor of a lovelorn spouse in relation to His consistently wayward people. Jeremiah writes, ". . . as a woman may betray her lover, so you have betrayed Me, house of Israel" (Jeremiah 3:20). God goes so far as to say that "unfaithful Israel had committed adultery" and He "had sent her away and had given her a certificate of divorce" (Jeremiah 3:8). The prophet Hosea had the unhappy task of literally acting out this role. These emotionally charged examples are how God feels about idolatry.

Fire represents passion, and the Lord is passionate about us. His zeal for His name and vehement reaction to idolatry are ultimately for our good. His jealousy springs out of His deep love for us. "Love's flames are fiery flames—the fiercest of all" (Song of Solomon 8:6).

In Revelation, John sees Jesus in his heavenly visions, "The Son of God, the One whose eyes are like a fiery flame" (Revelation 1:14; 2:18; 19:12). While certainly Christ has a gaze that pierces all and can see into people's hearts, I think it also speaks to the jealousy with which He looks upon His chosen people. Our wayward eyes drift from being fixed upon the source and perfecter of our faith (Hebrews 12:2). But His loving gaze burns with a passion for us that never grows cold.

Ravage or Refine

Visiting Sequoia National Forest in early spring is the closest experience to feeling like I was in Narnia. Most of the park was closed to vehicles as snow still blanketed the ground—contributing to the otherworldly sensation.

One will quickly notice the many trees with burn marks and charred stumps throughout the forest. We learned that forest fires regularly rage through the forest and that they are, in fact, essential to the life cycle of sequoias. Fires heat the cones of sequoias and cause them to release seeds while simultaneously recycling nutrients and preparing a seedbed for those sequoia seeds.

This is the striking duality of the nature of fire. Much like water, it can create or destroy—bring life or death.

This is certain: when fire shows up, change comes with it.

Context matters: Fire in a fireplace delights and warms. Fire outside of the fireplace wreaks havoc. One of the primary examples of this in the Bible has to do with our words. Passionate words lovingly spoken to a spouse delight. Scorching insults and rumors destroy. "Without wood, fire goes out, without a gossip, conflict dies down. As charcoal for embers and wood for fire, so is a quarrelsome man for kindling strife" (Proverbs 26:20–21). "A worthless man digs up evil, and his speech is like a scorching fire" (Proverbs 16:27).

In the New Testament, James has some strong language about our language:

> Consider how large a forest a small fire ignites. And the tongue is a fire. The tongue, a world of unrighteousness, is placed among the parts of our bodies. It pollutes the whole body, sets the course of life on fire, and is set on fire by hell.
> (James 3:5–6)

Our words have power. Just a few words—a small spark—can ignite a blaze that quickly grows out of control. We must use our words to bring light, life, and comfort.

Like the sequoias, sometimes we need fire in our lives. Fire tests us and can burn away unnecessary things in our lives—exposing our foundation which is Christ and teaching us that He truly is all we need (1 Corinthians 3:10–15).

The fire may be trials in this life like sickness or disaster. It could be persecution like Shadrach, Mesach, and Abednego whom Nebuchadnezzar had thrown into a blazing furnace heated "seven times more than was customary" (Daniel 3). But, remember, God promises to be with us and that "you will not be scorched when you walk through the fire, and the flame will not burn you" (Isaiah 43:2). This does not mean that we shall never suffer in this life, but disciples of Jesus should have no fear of men who can only harm the body but not the soul (Matthew 10:28).

The refining fire could come from the Lord who "does it for our benefit, so that we can share His holiness" (Hebrews 12:10). Pressure creates diamonds and fire refines gold. To get stronger muscles, we must apply mechanical tension. These are rules of life. God using life's "fires" to test and refine appears to be a ruling pattern as well.

In Isaiah 48, He says, "I have refined you, but not as silver; I have tested you in the furnace of affliction" (v. 10). Of the remnant of Israel in the last days, the prophet Zechariah writes:

> I will put this third through the fire;
> I will refine them as silver is refined
> and test them as gold is tested.
> They will call on My name,
> and I will answer them.
> I will say: They are My people,
> and they will say: Yahweh is our God.
> (Zechariah 13:9)

We should not only expect, but welcome, purifying fire and remember to look to and rely on God through it all. He is with us through all trials! As fire refines but also illuminates, so the Holy Spirit guides us on the journey of sanctification. When you encounter refining fires, lean into His help. Often, we come out of the fires with renewed life, richer soils of understanding, and a refined holiness gleaming a bit brighter.

Fire can refine and bring new life in our own lives, but it will also bring about the new creation. Like a phoenix rising from the ashes, creation will undergo a refining renovation. Since the fall, creation has been groaning under the burden of sin, waiting for the day it will be "set free from the bondage of corruption" (Romans 8:21–22). That day is coming soon.

Peter writes that the "present heavens and earth are stored up for fire, being kept until the day of judgment" (2 Peter 3:7). On that day, the "whole earth will be consumed by the fire of His jealousy" (Zephaniah 1:18). This is not a flood of water, but a flood of fire. "On that day the heavens will pass away with a loud noise, the elements will burn and be dissolved, and the earth and the works on it will be [burned up]" (2 Peter 3:10).

The dichotomous nature of fire will be on full display—the destruction of all that is unholy and, simultaneously, the refining renewal preparing the way for a new heaven and earth (2 Peter 3:13).

5

Blood Thicker than Water

My mistakes can never stop me, choice you make to adopt me,
The holes in your hands are the proof that you'll never drop me.

Andy Mineo[44]

A happy family is but an earlier heaven.

George Bernard Shaw

---

44 "Caught Dreaming." *Heroes For Sale*, by Andy Mineo. Reach Records, 2013.

Family is one of the few institutions created by God. It is the basis of all human relationships—the foundation of civilizations. It is therefore an important part of the Bible—especially in narrative writings. Family names, tribal belonging, and bloodlines were all central to the Israelites. Genealogies were carefully recorded and can be found in both the Old and New Testament. It turns out, familial terminology is one of the most commonly used in metaphorical language as well.

Individually, we are crafted in the image of God; however, there are some aspects of the Divine that are better understood through relationships. This is logical since we were created by a Triune God who is perpetually in communion with Himself. It is fascinating that God would design the basic familial frameworks of humanity in such a way that reveals more of His character.

We begin this chapter's journey in view of how we all begin life: as children.

Abba, Father

When the disciples asked Jesus to teach them how to pray, Jesus gave them a model prayer that starts with, "Our Father in heaven. . ." (Matthew 6:9–13; Luke 11:1–4). The Lord of heaven and earth is invoked as. . . Father?

(Of course, Jesus referred to God as His Father and to Himself as the Son throughout His earthly ministry. But Jesus also brought this language into His teaching of the disciples and the crowds.)

In the Sermon on the Mount, Jesus makes almost a dozen references to "your Heavenly Father" or "your Father in heaven."[45] Notice the *your* in each example except for the Lord's Prayer which starts with *our*. Jesus is talking to us!

It must have astonished the disciples to think of God in this way.

The Bible is clear that children are a gift. In fact, to be unable to have children was often considered by society as a form of divine punishment. There are many instances scattered throughout Scripture where God is depicted opening and closing the wombs

---

45 Some examples from the Sermon on the Mount: Matthew 5:16, 45, 48; 6:1, 9, 14, 26, 32; 7:11.

of women for various reasons. Consider references such as Genesis 20; 29:31-30:22, and Judges 13. From Isaac to Jesus, supernatural births are an uncanny theme.[46] Children are a miracle, and it is amazing that God uses this natural relationship to image supernatural truths.

The Old Testament is full of parental metaphors between God and His people. "When Israel was a child, I loved him, and out of Egypt I called My son" (Hosea 11:1). This verse contains prophecy fulfilled in Jesus; however, it also shows God as a loving Father. In Jeremiah 31, the Lord says, "I am Israel's Father" and "Isn't Ephraim a precious son to Me, a delightful child? Whenever I speak against him, I certainly still think about him. Therefore, My inner being yearns for him; I will truly have compassion on him" (vv. 9, 20).

There are even times where God compares Himself to a mother. To Israel, He says, "As a mother comforts her son, so I will comfort you" (Isaiah 66:13). And, "Can a woman forget her nursing child, or lack compassion for the child of her womb? Even if these forget, yet I will not forget you" (Isaiah 49:15). So, God is called our Father, but women are also made in His image and there is something about a mother's comfort and care that uniquely reflects God's character.

Unhappily, many references to Israel as children are not in a positive light. "They are a rebellious people, deceptive children, children who do not want to obey the LORD's instruction" (Isaiah 30:9). "Unfaithful children," and "obstinate and hardhearted" are just a few of the adjectives used by God (Deuteronomy 32:20; Ezekiel 2:4). These perverse patterns bring forth another fatherly attribute from God: discipline.

Since none of us is sinless, we all receive discipline. In fact, to not receive correction from our heavenly Father should be more worrisome. The writer of Hebrews tell us to:

> Endure suffering as discipline: God is dealing with you as sons. For what son is there that a father does not discipline? But if you are without discipline—which all receive—then you are illegitimate children and not sons.

---

46 Other examples include: Jacob, Joseph, Samson, Samuel, and John the Baptist.

Furthermore, we had natural fathers discipline us, and we respected them. Shouldn't we submit even more to the Father of spirits and live? For they disciplined us for a short time based on what seemed good to them, but He does it for our benefit, so that we can share His holiness. (Hebrews 12:7–10)

Our heavenly Father is perfect, and therefore even His discipline is perfect. It is not harsh and devoid of love, but rather flows out of His deep love. May we rejoice when we receive discipline, for it confirms our status as children and is molding us to become more like Him.

As a loving Father, God also gives His children good gifts. Yes, "every generous act and every perfect gift is from above, coming down from the Father" (James 1:17). Jesus uses a human hyperbole to make this point:

What man among you, if his son asks him for bread, will give him a stone? Or if he asks for a fish, will give him a snake? If you then, who are evil, know how to give good gifts to your children, how much more will your Father in heaven give good things to those who ask Him! (Matthew 7:9–11)

In context, Jesus is talking about prayer and directing us to keep asking, searching, and knocking. So, bring your requests! Your heavenly Father loves to give good gifts.

How amazing that, like little children, we can approach our Father in heaven. No formalities. No pretense. Like children, we can simply blurt out what is on our minds. Besides, He already knows it anyway.

Earlier in the Sermon on the Mount, Jesus says we are not to worry about physical things in life and that "your heavenly Father knows that you need them" (Matthew 6:32). Why should we ask if He already knows? Of course, asking acknowledges the reality that we are completely dependent on Him. But, also, He *wants* to hear from us. He cherishes a relationship with His children.

To communicate with our heavenly Father is an act of faith.

Childlike faith is praised by Jesus. In two different instances with the disciples, Jesus makes this clear. When they ask, "Who is the greatest in the kingdom of heaven?" Jesus replies:

> Unless you are converted and become like children, you will never enter the kingdom of heaven. Therefore, whoever humbles himself like this child—this one is the greatest in the kingdom of heaven. And whoever welcomes one child like this in My name welcomes Me. (Matthew 18:1–5)

Later, when the disciples try to prevent people from bringing their children before Jesus, He tells them to "leave the children alone, and don't try to keep them from coming to Me, because the kingdom of heaven is made up of people like this" (Matthew 19:14). Humility, trust, and an almost naïve boldness are the marks of childlike faith.

The psalmist describes this posture:

> LORD, my heart is not proud;
> my eyes are not haughty.
> I do not get involved with things
> too great or too difficult for me.
>
> Instead, I have calmed and quieted myself
> like a little weaned child with its mother;
> I am like a little child.
> (Psalm 131:1–2)

When we approach our heavenly Father with this kind of faith, He is ready to meet us with faithful love. "As a father has compassion on his children, so the LORD has compassion on those who fear Him" (Psalm 103:13). He will never leave or forsake us. He does not make mistakes as we humans do. Even if our earthly father or mother abandons us, the Lord cares for us (Psalm 27:10). He always keeps His promises.

How does one become a part of this heavenly household?

We cannot be naturally born into this family.
We have to be reborn.
We have to be adopted.

Adoption

> When the time came to completion, God sent His Son, born of a woman, born under the law, to redeem those under the law, so that we might receive adoption as sons. And because you are sons, God has sent the Spirit of His Son into our hearts, crying, "Abba, Father!" So you are no longer a slave but a son, and if a son, then an heir through God.
> (Galatians 4:4–7)

No earthly privilege or social standing can get one into this spiritual family. No ethnicity nor royal bloodline. To the Pharisees and Sadducees Jesus said, "Don't presume to say to yourselves, 'We have Abraham as our father.' For I tell you that God is able to raise up children for Abraham from these stones!" (Matthew 3:9). Not even being a descendent of Abraham grants access to this family.

As Jesus was teaching, some in the crowd said His mother and brothers were outside, wanting to speak with Him. His response, at first glance, seems rather harsh:

> But He replied to the one who told Him, "Who is My mother and who are My brothers?" And stretching out His hand toward His disciples, He said, "Here are My mother and My brothers! For whoever does the will of My Father in heaven, that person is My brother and sister and mother."
> (Matthew 12:48–50)

Is Jesus disowning His mother and brothers? Of course not. But it shows, by comparison, the great significance of this spiritual family.

Adoption into this family comes with new brothers and sisters, among whom Jesus is the firstborn Son.

The first time we see the theme of the firstborn is in Genesis when Abel presents an offering to the Lord—"some of the firstborn of his flock" (Genesis 4:4). The firstborn position was of unique importance—especially in respect to inheritance. The firstborn of man and animal belonged to the Lord (Exodus 13:2; Leviticus 27:26; Luke 2:23). A redemption price had to be paid for firstborn sons and unclean animals which pointed back to when the Lord struck down the firstborn sons in the final plague (Numbers 18:15–17). Israel is even referred to as God's firstborn (Exodus 4:22; Jeremiah 31:9).

Jesus is the fulfillment of all these patterns. He is "the firstborn over all creation. For everything was created by Him" and "the firstborn from the dead, so that He might come to have first place in everything" (Colossians 1:15–18). With Christ as the firstborn, the rest of the believers are all spiritual siblings (Romans 8:29). There is a name for this special family: the church.

Much can be said on what the Bible says the church should look like, but we will predominantly focus on viewing the church as a family and the characteristics of oneness, discipleship, and love seen through that lens.

Of critical importance in areas rife with persecution, adoption into the church can mean one gaining a new family when disowned by one's natural family. It can even mean the difference between life and death. What a beautiful picture of adoptive love—to take in new believers forsaken by their earthly family.

Love is to be the defining characteristic of the church family. Jesus Himself said, "By this all people will know that you are My disciples, if you have love for one another" (John 13:35). We are to "show family affection to one another with brotherly love" (Romans 12:10). Love is even how we discern who are true members of the family. "This is how God's children—and the Devil's children—are made evident. Whoever does not do what is right is not of God, especially the one who does not love his brother" (1 John 3:10).

This affection within the church is intended to be beautiful to behold in both its diversity and oneness. The church is diverse in the makeup of individuals and yet of one accord under the umbrella of the gospel. Like the most exquisite solitaire diamond is a single diamond, yet scintillates beautifully in the light with its multifaceted design, so is a properly functioning church.

The diversity of the church family stretches across all language, race, ethnicity, age, and socioeconomic strata. Indeed, it even stretches across time itself—this is an eternal family. In John's vision of heaven, he sees "a vast multitude from every nation, tribe, people, and language, which no one could number, standing before the throne and before the Lamb" (Revelation 7:9). Heaven is not colorblind! As a diamond will glimmer with different colors, there is something about every culture uniquely sparkling in reflection of the Imago Dei.

This diversity was not a mistake on God's part. In fact, it is intentional and is seen in how the church is meant to function together. Paul uses the analogy of a body with different body parts. "For as the body is one and has many parts, and all the parts of that body, though many, are one body—so also is Christ" (1 Corinthians 12:12). Diversity in how the Spirit distributes spiritual gifts underscores how necessary it is that the church be a community working together.

> Speaking the truth in love, let us grow in every way into Him who is the head—Christ. From Him the whole body, fitted and knit together by every supporting ligament, promotes the growth of the body for building up itself in love by the proper working of each individual part. (Ephesians 4:15–16)

So, ingeniously, as individuals lean into their unique giftings and abilities, it simultaneously builds up the church as a unified family. The diversity of the church family of Christ should enrich the body internally while an external world looks on with bewildered attraction at how such a patchwork of people love one another so well.

Although the individual roles are important, Christ is the head of the body. To look more like Him and to share His love is the end goal. No individual attribute is to ever usurp the centrality of Christ. For "there are different gifts, but the same Spirit. There are different ministries, but the same Lord. And there are different activities, but the same God activates each gift in each person" (1 Corinthians 12:4–6).

To maintain and grow in this synchronous unity-and-diversity dance takes work—not because it doesn't work, but rather because our selfishness and sin get in the way. Joni Eareckson Tada says this well: "Believers are never told to become one; we already are one and are expected to act like it."[47] Paul knew this as well, saying that this work takes humility, patience, and gentleness, and that we must be diligent to keep "the unity of the Spirit with the peace that binds us" (Ephesians 4:1–3). He reminds us that:

> There is one body and one Spirit—just as you were called to one hope at your calling—one Lord, one faith, one baptism, one God and Father of all, who is above all and through all and in all.
> (Ephesians 4:4–6)

While our diversity sparkles, the unifying characteristic that holds the family together is our adoption. For "in Christ there is not Greek and Jew, circumcision and uncircumcision, barbarian, Scythian, slave and free; but Christ is all and in all" (Colossians 3:11). Similarly, Paul writes to the Galatians: "There is no Jew or Greek, slave or free, male or female; for you are all one in Christ Jesus" (Galatians 3:28). The gospel flows in our reborn veins. The blood of Christ is our unbreakable bond.

Orphans hear nothing of the words "estate planning." But Jesus said He would not leave us as orphans (John 14:18)—we are adopted! Did you know that now, as a son or daughter of the King, you will receive an inheritance?

When we move from death to life—from children under wrath to children of our heavenly Father—we receive the Holy Spirit. "He is the down payment of our inheritance, for the redemption of the possession, to the praise of His glory" (Ephesians 1:14). "The Spirit Himself testifies together with our spirit that we are God's children, and if children, also heirs—heirs of God and co-heirs with Christ" (Romans 8:16–17). Brothers and sisters, we are

---

47 https://www.ligonier.org/learn/articles/spontaneous-compassion (originally published in Tabletalk magazine).

co-heirs with Christ!

In Revelation 5, God is seated on His throne and holds a scroll in His right hand. It has writing on the front and back and seven seals. No one in the universe is found worthy to open it. What is this document of such importance?

It is "God's will, his final settlement of the affairs of the universe."[48]

Jesus, simultaneously Lion of Judah and Lamb of God, is the only one worthy to break the seals and open the scroll.

> What none of the whole human race were found competent to do, Christ in the character of 'the Lamb' does. In His own person he claims the inheritance, asserts His right to 'the possession' which He 'purchased,' and to which in man's nature He has for man established a new title. He took on Him human nature for this very purpose.[49]

As a co-heir with Christ, did you know you are included in God's will?

All of the portion, possession, and purchasing language point to this coming crescendo of history as we know it.[50] Our inheritance is to be Christ's inheritance—"a people for His possession" (1 Peter 2:9). The Lord is our portion and we are His. We can proclaim with the psalmist: "Indeed, I have a beautiful inheritance!" (Psalm 16:6).

The Holy Spirit is the "down payment of our inheritance, for the redemption of the possession, to the praise of His glory" (Ephesians 1:14; see also 2 Corinthians 1:22; 5:5). And this is not a transactional contract. It is a covenant. What Christ has purchased with His blood, He will fully redeem! Nothing shall stop God from bequeathing all blessings upon the Son and His church.

---

48   In the Roman empire, wills had seven seals.

49   William De Burgh, *An Exposition of the Book of Revelation*, Hodges, Smith, & Company, 1857.

50   This inheritance language is found all over the pages of Scripture. It is a worthy exploration. One place to start is Jeremiah 32 where Jeremiah is told by God to redeem his uncle's land.

The glorious future reality of this inheritance in the light—where we are wholly His people and He is wholly our God—fits perfectly with our final familial symbol.

Profound Mystery

"Zebra, emu, platypus. . ." As Adam was giving names to all of the animals, "no helper was found as his complement" (Genesis 2:20). From the beginning, we were built for relationships with other humans. The Lord God said, "It is not good for the man to be alone. I will make a helper as his complement" (Genesis 2:18). Out of Adam's rib, God crafted a woman—His final act of creation before calling it all "very good" and taking a Sabbath—and presented her to Adam. God officiated the first wedding, Adam burst into poetic joy, and there was the very first marriage.

As a fundamental institution created by God, marriage is the foundational building block of families—of civilization itself. Adam named his wife Eve because she was the mother of all people (Genesis 3:20). It is also foundational to understanding deeper spiritual realities. The Bible is rich with marriage metaphors.

The Lord uses the covenantal language of marriage in relation to His chosen people of Israel. To them God says, "Your husband is your Maker—His name is Yahweh of Hosts" (Isaiah 54:5). As we shall see, in every example God is compared to the husband and His people to the bride. Like marriage, this relationship is a covenant. And, although God always keeps His promises, His imperfect people do not.

Speaking through the prophet Jeremiah, the Lord says:

> Can a young woman forget her jewelry
> or a bride her wedding sash?
> Yet My people have forgotten Me
> for countless days.
>
> However, as a woman may betray her lover,
> so you have betrayed Me, house of Israel.
> This is the LORD's declaration.
> (Jeremiah 2:32, 3:20)

The emotionally charged language captures God's heart for His people. A stunning example of this metaphor is the entire book of Hosea. Imagine your calling as a prophet starting like this. . .

When the LORD first spoke to Hosea, He said this to him:

> Go and marry a promiscuous wife
> and have children of promiscuity,
> for the land is committing blatant acts of promiscuity
> by abandoning the LORD.
> (Hosea 1:2)

Throughout the rest of the book, the drama unfolds as Hosea must love an unfaithful woman—even chasing her down and buying her back—just as God does with His people.

The severity of Israel's idolatrous behavior reflects in the language of divorce used by God.

This is what the LORD says:

> Where is your mother's divorce certificate
> that I used to send her away?
> Or who were My creditors that I sold you to?
> Look, you were sold for your iniquities,
> and your mother was put away
> because of your transgressions.
> (Isaiah 50:1)

Just as unfaithfulness devastates human marriages, idolatry destroys our relationship with the Lord. God says, "It was because unfaithful Israel had committed adultery that I had sent her away and had given her a certificate of divorce" (Jeremiah 3:8).

If you have gone through the dark depths of divorce, know that we[51] do not have a God who is unable to sympathize with us. He knows what it feels like to be rejected and forgotten. He knows—surely in a deeper sense than we can imagine—the experience of being cheated, lied to, or abandoned. Our Lord knows what heartache is.

---

51 When I say "we," I am personally included in this demographic.

However, unlike mere humans, the Lord still lovingly pursues us. Indeed, His thoughts are not our thoughts and His ways higher than our ways (Isaiah 55:8–9). Yes, even "if we are faithless, He remains faithful, for He cannot deny Himself" (2 Timothy 2:13). Our story has a happily ever after.

> You will no longer be called Deserted,
> and your land will not be called Desolate;
> instead, you will be called My Delight is in Her,
> and your land Married;
> for the LORD delights in you,
> and your land will be married.
> For as a young man marries a young woman,
> so your sons will marry you;
> and as a groom rejoices over his bride,
> so your God will rejoice over you.
> (Isaiah 62:4–5)

The Lord redeems us, restores us, and even rejoices over us! What magnificent marriage language describing His steadfast love.

> I will take you to be My wife forever.
> I will take you to be My wife in righteousness,
> justice, love, and compassion.
> I will take you to be My wife in faithfulness,
> and you will know Yahweh.
> (Hosea 2:19–20)

These are the Lord's vows—His promises. When He says something will come to pass, then nothing shall prevent it.

We continue to see marriage imagery in the New Testament. The metaphor is consistent as God is the groom and His people are the bride; however, now we have new covenant terms: Christ and the church.

John the Baptist referred to himself as a groomsman who rejoices greatly at the voice of the groom—referring to Jesus (John 3:27–30). When asked why His disciples did not fast, Jesus replied, "Can the wedding guests be sad while the groom is with them? The time will come when the groom will be taken away from them, and then they will fast" (Matthew 9:15; see also Mark 2:19; Luke 5:32).

In His teachings, Jesus used many parables related to weddings. There is the parable of the wedding banquet (Matthew 22:1–14) or the parable of the Ten Virgins (Matthew 25:1–13).

While speaking about marriage in his letter to the Ephesian church, Paul invokes this same imagery:

> Wives, submit to your own husbands *as to the Lord*, for the husband is the head of the wife as *Christ is the head of the church. He is the Savior of the body*. Now as *the church submits to Christ*, so wives are to submit to their husbands in everything. Husbands, love your wives, *just as Christ loved the church and gave Himself for her to make her holy*, cleansing her with the washing of water by the word. *He did this to present the church to Himself in splendor*, without spot or wrinkle or anything like that, but holy and blameless. In the same way, husbands are to love their wives as their own bodies. He who loves his wife loves himself. For no one ever hates his own flesh but provides and cares for it, *just as Christ does for the church, since we are members of His body*.
>
> For this reason a man will leave
> his father and mother
> and be joined to his wife,
> and the two will become one flesh.
>
> *This mystery is profound, but I am talking about Christ and the church.*
> (Ephesians 5:22–32)

So, we see that God embedded truths about spiritual realities in the physical human institution of marriage.

Paul extrapolates principles that we can learn from the relationship between Christ and His church and its application to how husbands and wives should interact. But what does this profound mystery say about the relationship of believers with Christ in eternity? How do these truths play out when "in the resurrection they neither marry nor are given in marriage but are like angels in heaven" (Matthew 22:30)?

We do know that there will be a wedding in heaven. In John's vision of heaven, he sees the preparation of a grand wedding celebration.

> Let us be glad, rejoice, and give Him glory,
> because the marriage of the Lamb has come,
> and His wife has prepared herself.
> She was given fine linen to wear, bright and pure. For the
> fine linen represents the righteous acts of the saints.
> (Revelation 19:7–8)

John also describes an angel saying to him: "'Come, I will show you the bride, the wife of the Lamb.' He then carried [John] away in the Spirit to a great and high mountain and showed [him] the holy city, Jerusalem, coming down out of heaven from God" (Revelation 21:9–10).

This is the magnificent marriage of God and His people. As John's vision shows both the twelve tribes of Israel and the twelve names of the Lamb's apostles inscribed upon the new Jerusalem, this bride is made up of all of the saints from all of history.

The bride descends from heaven—signifying she is not of human beauty, glory, or handiwork. It is God who prepares her and bestows His radiant glory upon her. It is God who makes us beautiful (Ezekiel 16:8–14).

And to what end does God do all these things? Clearly, we benefit. Ultimately, it is for Himself. Our glorification is for His glory. This purpose shows up in two phrases that the Lord repeats dozens of times in the Old Testament: "Then they will know that I am Yahweh" and "They will be My people and I will be their God."

After John sees Jerusalem coming down out of heaven "prepared like a bride adorned for her husband," he hears a loud voice from the heavenly throne say:

> Look! God's dwelling is with humanity,
> and He will live with them.
> They will be His people,
> and God Himself will be with them
> and be their God.
> (Revelation 21:2–3)

The word used to describe dwelling is literally "tabernacled." It is a word that only shows up in John's writings.[52] It is a word rich with allusion to the Tabernacle of the Old Testament where the presence of the Lord dwelt. It is a word that goes beyond simply occupying the same space—it is far more intimate.

This is the marriage between the Lamb and His bride—between Christ and His church—when the veil of the curse is lifted and our redemption complete. The Tabernacle of God shall be with men, and He will tabernacle with them. Then there will be the final realization of the name Immanuel—God with us!—a union between God and His people never previously known; a level of currently unimaginable intimacy with our Lord; a grand consummation.

The saints will *know* the Lord. Yet, this joyful knowing shall continue to blossom for an eternity. Our sublime—or dare I say, orgasmic—pleasure will be to forever know more deeply what is "the length and width, height and depth of God's love" (Ephesians 3:18). A blissful intercourse of which the delights of earthly marriage are merely a foretaste—a profound mystery.

---

52 John uses this language in only five verses. All of the implied allusions to the Tabernacle, Temple, and that the Word became flesh are worthy of exploration. See John 1:14; Revelation 7:15, 12:12, 13:6, 21:3.

6

The Mark on Their Foreheads

*The only freedom that man ever has is when he becomes
a slave to Jesus Christ.*

R. C. Sproul

*Jesus came to give good news and to set the captives free (Amen)
Jesus came for the poor (Amen)
Jesus came with the keys (Amen)
Jesus came to remove the chains so the prisoners are released*

Flame, "Start Over"[53]

---

53   "Start Over." *Royal Flush*, by Flame. Clear Sight Music, 2013.

S lavery is a sad subject. Unfortunately, it is also as old as humanity. The theme of slavery is a recurring story in Israel's
history and, as we shall see, it is pertinent to all of our lives both
practically and spiritually.

Exodus

Israel's subservient time in Egypt was a defining theme in the
lives of the Israelites. From the feast of Passover to weekly Sabbath rest, their rhythms of life harkened back to this time period
out of which God rescued them.

And God reminded them often of this fact saying, "I am Yahweh your God, who brought you out of the land of Egypt, so that
you would no longer be their slaves. I broke the bars of your yoke
and enabled you to live in freedom" (Leviticus 26:13). Even at the
start of the Ten Commandments, God says He is the One "who
brought you out of the land of Egypt, out of the place of slavery"
(Exodus 20:2).

Israel's slavery is a shadow of a more sinister form that has
plagued every human since the fall.

The Law of Fealty

*It is ordained in the eternal constitution of things, that men of
intemperate minds cannot be free. Their passions forge their
fetters.*
Edmund Burke

Make no mistake—every one of us serves a master. A synonymous
word for serve is worship. Pastor and author Paul David Tripp el-
oquently sums up this aspect of human nature:

> Human beings by their very nature are worshipers. Wor-
> ship is not something we do; it defines who we are. You
> cannot divide human beings into those who worship and
> those who don't. Everybody worships; it's just a matter of
> what, or whom, we serve.[54]

---

54 Paul David Tripp, *Instruments in the Redeemer's Hands: People in Need of*

What we worship will obtain our obedience. The object of our worship will capture our attention, drive our choices, and mold our character. This is the Law of Fealty.

Ever since the world fell under the curse of sin and death, we humans, by default, have been enslaved to our selfish sin nature. We are under sin's dominion. Lest we be too quick to think of ourselves as above such a predicament, let us consider a conversation Jesus had with the Jews:

> So Jesus said to the Jews who had believed Him, "If you continue in My word, you really are My disciples. You will know the truth, and the truth will set you free."
>
> "We are descendants of Abraham," they answered Him, "and we have never been enslaved to anyone. How can You say, 'You will become free'?"
>
> Jesus responded, "I assure you: Everyone who commits sin is a slave of sin.
> (John 8:31–34)

In their pride and selfishness, these Jews clearly suffered from voluntary amnesia in saying they had never been enslaved to anyone. Israel had been slaves in Egypt and Babylon, and the Jews talking with Jesus were themselves under the oppressive reign of the Roman empire. Jesus says everyone who commits sin is a slave of sin. All have sinned and fall short of the glory of God (Romans 3:23). Therefore, *all* are under sin's domain, "sold into sin's power" (Romans 7:14). To arrogantly believe we sit on the throne of our own lives is folly.

There is a war being waged for our worship. The powers of darkness—through the world, via the flaming arrows of the devil, or by way of our sinful flesh—want to ensnare us. What did the devil truly want during the temptation of Jesus in the wilderness? He wanted Jesus to worship him (Matthew 4:9). Why? John Piper explains it this way:

Change Helping People in Need of Change (Phillipsburg, NJ: P&R Publishing, 2002).

What Satan sees rightly is that the one who is worshiped over all is the one for whom all exists. . . . If I worship you for giving me the nations, then I acknowledge that the nations exist for your sake. Letting Jesus have world rulership would not have been a loss for Satan, if Jesus ruled the world for Satan's sake. And that is what worship means. It means that Jesus would acknowledge Satan as his greatest allegiance and greatest treasure.[55]

Satan wants our fealty. And he wants to keep us enslaved to sin. As God told Cain, "Sin is crouching at the door. Its desire is for you" (Genesis 4:7). We can feel this battle inside. We know all too well what Paul is describing in his letter to the Romans:

> So I discover this principle: When I want to do what is good, evil is with me. For in my inner self I joyfully agree with God's law. But I see a different law in the parts of my body, *waging war* against the law of my mind and *taking me prisoner* to the law of sin in the parts of my body. (Romans 7:21–23)

We can feel the weight of these spiritual shackles. And in chorus with Paul we exclaim, "What a wretched person I am! Who will rescue me from this dying body?" (Romans 7:24).

Liberty to the Captives

How do you change your behavior? Change what you worship.
Tim Keller[56]

As Paul's question at the end of Romans 7 implies, our freedom from sin's shackles lies not in some*thing* but some*one*—Jesus. He is our Savior and Lord. He is our Savior, in that He has broken the chains of sin and death and "has rescued us from the domain of

55   John Piper, *Come, Lord Jesus: Meditations on the Second Coming of Christ* (Wheaton, IL: Crossway, 2023), 50.
56   https://x.com/timkellernyc/status/1459177669501849619

darkness" (Colossians 1:13); He is our Lord, in that He is now our Master. True freedom is found in slavery to our Savior.

Jesus made clear His divine rescue mission. While in His hometown of Nazareth on a Sabbath, Jesus proclaimed in the synagogue that He was the fulfillment of the words of the prophet Isaiah:

> The Spirit of the Lord God is on Me,
> because the Lord has anointed Me
> to bring good news to the poor.
> He has sent Me to heal the brokenhearted,
> to proclaim liberty to the captives
> and freedom to the prisoners.
> (Isaiah 61:1)

This is the gospel—that, through the death and resurrection of Jesus, we really can be set free! As the contemporary theologian N. T. Wright puts it:

> He has done it. With Jesus, God's rescue operation has been put into effect once and for all. A great door has swung open in the cosmos which can never again be shut. It's the door to the prison where we've been kept chained up. We are offered freedom: freedom to experience God's rescue for ourselves, to go through the open door and explore the new world to which we now have access.[57]

In a beautiful bewilderment, the Lord of heaven and earth humbled Himself as a slave in order to save us. With unmatched meekness, Jesus:

> Who, existing in the form of God,
> did not consider equality with God
> as something to be used for His own advantage.
> Instead He emptied Himself
> by *assuming the form of a slave,*

---

57   N. T. Wright, *Simply Christian: Why Christianity Makes Sense* (San Francisco: HarperOne, 2010), 92.

> taking on the likeness of men.
> And when He had come as a man
> in His external form,
> He humbled Himself by becoming obedient
> to the point of death—
> even to death on a cross.
> (Philippians 2:6–8)

We have an eternally gracious God who would step out of the glorious and holy heavens and stoop down into our filthy and depraved prison. Not only that, but He would take our place.

Like Barabbas,[58] we are released and Jesus takes upon Himself our due punishment. Indeed, we were "bought at a price" (1 Corinthians 6:20, 7:23)—of incalculable cost!

When we are purchased by the blood of Christ, we are liberated from sin and become enslaved to God (Romans 6:22). Peter calls Christians "God's slaves" (1 Peter 2:16). Paul introduces himself as a "slave" and "prisoner" of Chris Jesus throughout his letters (some examples: Romans 1:1; Galatians 1:10; Philemon 1:1). Both Jude[59] and James refer to themselves as slaves of Jesus (James 1:1; Jude 1:1). Even the angels adopt this vocabulary. In John's Revelation, he falls down at the feet of an angel, but the angel responds, "Don't do that! *I am a fellow slave* with you and your brothers who have the testimony about Jesus" (Revelation 19:10).

There is another fascinating piece of symbolism in Scripture that relates to the theme of slavery we shall explore next.

Let it be a Symbol on Your Forehead

Throughout human history, symbols have been used to communicate ownership. When countries conquered new lands, one of the first acts was to raise their flag—signifying to the rest of the

---

58   The name Barabbas literally means "son of a father." This rather generic name could almost be interpreted as "someone." And all peoples are sons / daughters of a father. Jesus, the Son of the Father, takes the place of all peoples.

59   Jude also identifies himself as the brother of James—the leader of the Jerusalem church and (half) brother of Jesus. Therefore, a brother that likely initially scoffed at Jesus (John 7:1–9) now humbly labeled himself His slave.

world that they now lay claim to that piece of geography. When ranchers brand cattle, they physically emblazon an emblem displaying to whom those animals belong.

Unfortunately, humans also repeatedly abuse assignment of symbols in order to seek ownership over that which is never rightfully theirs—other people. Mesopotamian branding and tattooing of slaves is well documented. These marks would signify service to a human master or even pagan deity, in the case of temple slaves. Egyptian, Greek, and Roman records show the prevalence of "inscribed" slaves. In modern times, one cannot help but think of the atrocities of the Nazi concentration camps where serial numbers were tattooed onto prisoners for identification.

On a more positive note, individuals will voluntarily place a mark on themselves of religious significance. A bindi is the common decorative colored dot worn on the forehead, primarily by Hindus. It is supposed to represent the "third eye" or location of the "sixth chakra," representing concealed wisdom. On Ash Wednesday, which marks the start of the season of Lent, Christians around the world (more typical in Orthodox and Catholic traditions) will draw a cross on their foreheads with ashes. This symbolizes mortality (ashes to ashes, dust to dust) and repentance.

It is noteworthy that these practices, in particular, involve placing a symbol on the forehead. There is a Jewish practice that incorporates the forehead.

In Deuteronomy 6, we find the most famous portion of The Shema,[60] one of the main passages of core Jewish beliefs. Part of the instruction in this passage is to remember God's words and

---

60   The Shema is technically made up of three passages: Deuteronomy 6:4–9, 11:13–21; and Numbers 15:37–41. This collection of verses is where the Jewish customs of tefillin, mezuzah (affixing small containers containing scrolls of Scripture to doorposts), and tzitzit (tassels with a blue cord at the corners of garments) are derived from.

Traditionally, the Shema would be recited at least twice per day—once upon waking and once at bedtime. The Shema is used during the high holy day of Yom Kippur. Devout Jews even recite it when they believe they are on their deathbed.

When the Pharisees and Sadducees tested Jesus by asking Him which command was the greatest, ironically, Jesus quoted part of the Shema—Scripture they undoubtedly recited multiple times per day, yet failed miserably in understanding and carrying out.

"bind them as a sign on your hand and let them be a symbol on your forehead" (Deuteronomy 6:8). This type of command is repeated in several other Old Testament passages (for example, Deuteronomy 11:18; Exodus 13:9, 16). While most commentators submit that this was metaphoric language, in typical Israelite fashion, they interpreted it literally. Hence, we have the Jewish practice of tefillin (or phylacteries).

Tefillin are two black leather straps with boxes containing parchments of Scripture. One is to be placed on the arm and the other on the forehead. The clear meaning is the Lord and His words are to be always on our minds and are to guide our every action.

Jesus referred to this practice in His denouncing of the hypocritical scribes and Pharisees:

> They tie up heavy loads that are hard to carry and put them on people's shoulders, but they themselves aren't willing to lift a finger to move them. They do everything to be observed by others: They enlarge their phylacteries and lengthen their tassels.
> (Matthew 23:4–5)

In His usual modus operandi, Jesus cuts to the heart of the matter. To quote the theologian J I Packer, "There is nothing more irreligious than self-absorbed religion."[61] The Pharisees were manipulatively serving themselves, not the "one Master, the Messiah" (Matthew 23:10).

The religious practice of tefillin is intended to be an outward sign that the wearers serve God with all their heart, soul, and strength (Deuteronomy 6:5). The symbol on their forehead proclaims to whom they belong. As we shall see, this is not the last time in Scripture we observe this pattern.

In Ezekiel's vision of the Babylonian destruction of Jerusalem,[62] he sees a man dressed in linen with a writing kit at his side. The Lord instructs the one clothed in linen to pass through the

---

61 J. I. Packer, *Knowing God* (London: Hodder and Stoughton, 1973), 36.

62 Of course, Ezekiel's vision came true. The carnage in chapter nine is recorded in 2 Chronicles 36:17–19. Both passages point to God using Babylon to execute His divine judgment. The Lord is sovereign and always in control of history.

city and "put a mark on the foreheads of the men who sigh and groan over all the detestable practices committed in it" (Ezekiel 9:4). Those with the mark had demonstrated their fealty to God and were protected from the subsequent slaughter.

A dramatic demarcation shall take place in the last days. As Jesus said, "No one can be a slave of two masters, since either he will hate one and love the other, or be devoted to one and despise the other" (Matthew 6:24). In context, Jesus is talking about serving and worshiping God versus riches; however, the same principle can be applied to any "master" that seeks to usurp God's rightful and exclusive position. There is either serving Christ or denying Him. There is no middle ground. There is no third option.

As pastor and author Dane Ortlund writes:

> If we never come to him, we will experience a judgment so fierce it will be like a double-edged sword coming out of his mouth at us (Rev. 1:16; 2:12; 19:15, 21). If we do come to him, as fierce as his lion-like judgment would have been against us, so deep will be his lamb-like tenderness for us (cf. Rev. 5:5–6; Isa. 40:10–11). We will be enveloped in one or the other. To no one will Jesus be neutral.[63]

This is the choice presented to humanity in the end of days: to exalt the Lamb or to become a bondservant of the beast.

Between the sixth and seventh opening of the seals on the heavenly scroll, God places a mark on those who follow Him:

> Then I saw another angel, who had the seal of the living God rise up from the east. He cried out in a loud voice to the four angels who were empowered to harm the earth and the sea: "Don't harm the earth or the sea or the trees until we seal the slaves of our God on their foreheads." And I heard the number of those who were sealed:
>
> 144,000 sealed from every tribe of the Israelites (Revelation 7:2–4)

---

63 Dane Ortlund, *Gentle and Lowly: The Heart of Christ for Sinners and Sufferers* (Wheaton, IL: Crossway, 2020), 54.

And what was this mark on their foreheads? We find out in Revelation 14 where John sees them next to the Lamb with "His name and His Father's name written on their foreheads" (Revelation 14:1). Like the mark in Ezekiel's vision, this one protects its recipients from harm.

Satan cannot create. He can only imitate, deceive, and destroy.[64] His puppet, the beast (or antichrist), forces the inhabitants of earth to receive his mark:

> And he requires everyone—small and great, rich and poor, free and slave—to be given a mark on his right hand or on his forehead, so that no one can buy or sell unless he has the mark: the beast's name or the number of his name.

> Here is wisdom: The one who has understanding must calculate the number of the beast, because it is the number of a man. His number is 666.
> (Revelation 13:16–18)

While much attention has been given to the number 666,[65] it is clear that this mark perversely parallels the meanings of the Shema, tefillin, and God's seal on His followers. In this case, it is Satan who seeks all worship, devotion, and dominion. Those who refuse the mark of the beast cannot conduct business and will be subject to death.

So, to receive a mark is to be branded but it also broadcasts branding. In the business world, "brand identity" is a popular term to describe what a brand stands for. For example, if I say

---

64   Satan concocts his own malevolent mimicry of God in the end times in order to deceive the world with his own "unholy trinity." It consists of himself (the dragon), the antichrist (the beast), and the false prophet.

65   What is certainly the most (in)famous number in all of the Bible, 666, has been a topic of debate and fascination in both theological circles and popular culture. Personally, I lean towards the symbolic definition that the number six falls short of seven—being the number of perfection. The six repeated three times represents absolute imperfection in a similar, but contrasting way, that "holy" is the only characteristic of God repeated three times (see the chapter "Fractals & Echoes" for more on numbers in Scripture). In any case, I will be the first to admit I have not the wisdom John refers to for deciphering such things, and I believe the antichrist will be made plain to those who have "eyes to see" at that time in history.

"Ferrari" and "Volvo," we picture two very different types of consumers driving each brand of car. In a way, people choose brands that advertise *who they are*. It is an exhibition of public identity.

While we may not endure the choice of receiving or refusing the mark of the beast, we all face the same choice spiritually. "Don't you know that. . . you are slaves of that one you obey—either of sin leading to death or of obedience leading to righteousness?" (Romans 6:16).

What do the "marks" in our lives say about whom we worship? Our habits, schedules, and priorities? What statement would our bank statement make?

To quote the wizard Saruman in *The Lord of the Rings*: "Whom do you serve?"

Freedom in Christ

The Law of Freedom

We have established that Jesus sets us free "from the law of sin and of death" (Romans 8:2). Indeed, "Where the Spirit of the Lord is, there is freedom" (2 Corinthians 3:17). Hallelujah! Now, what does it look like to now walk in this freedom? How do we view and experience this freedom during our "temporary residence" (1 Peter 1:17) with its trials and sufferings that "are not worth comparing with the glory that is going to be revealed to us" (Romans 8:18)? We come now to the Law of Freedom.

In James' letter, he tells believers to "be doers of the word and not hearers only" (James 1:22). He describes people who hear the word without doing like people who gaze at themselves in a mirror, walk away, and immediately forget what they look like. Continuing with this thought, he says, "But the one who looks intently into the perfect law of freedom and perseveres in it, and is not a forgetful hearer but one who does good works—this person will be blessed in what he does" (James 1:25). Later in his letter, James instructs Christians to "speak and act as those who will be judged by the law of freedom" (v. 12).

How is it that law and freedom are placed together? It sounds like an oxymoron.

We find another paradox in Jesus' teachings that relates to our present theme: "The last shall be first and the first shall be last" (Luke 18:14). If you want to be great in the kingdom of heaven, you must humble yourself (Matthew 18:4).

Jesus did not simply teach this—He exemplified it. As Jesus knew the crucifixion was drawing near, He was at supper with His disciples and washed their feet. Foot washing was a normal practice in a day and age where most walked on dirt roads in sandals. But, this task was considered so dirty and lowly that it was only done by non-Jewish slaves.[66] Jesus then told His disciples that He was giving them an example in humility and service to follow (John 13:13–15).

We often think about Jesus' astonishing servant leadership during His incarnate time on earth, but do we consider it continuing on into eternity? Luke records a remarkable parable that Jesus told:

> You must be like people waiting for their master to return
> from the wedding banquet so that when he comes and
> knocks, they can open the door for him at once. Those
> slaves the master will find alert when he comes will be
> blessed. I assure you: He will get ready, have them recline
> at the table, then come and serve them.
> (Luke 12:36–37)

Here, believers are the slaves that are to be watchful for the Master's return. His return is Jesus' second coming (see verse 40 in context). Then we see the twist—the paradox: The Master, Jesus, does not sit down to be served but instead serves us, believers!

What? This is a mind-boggling image! Jesus will serve us in heaven?

Well, if the one who is the most humble and has the most "last-ness" shall be first, then Jesus clearly claims that place. Certainly, He is the first—preeminent and above all. Faithful love and grace

---

66   All twelve disciples are still with Jesus at this point, but He does hint at the fact that one of them will betray Him (John 13:2–3, 10–11) Even with this foreknowledge, Jesus washes Judas Iscariot's feet.

are in His nature. And if it is His grace that saves and preserves us on this side of eternity, will it not be His limitless grace that is lavished upon us and keeps us forevermore? Yes, those slaves are surely blessed!

So, Jesus is showing us how the kingdom functions and the path to true freedom. If the Law of Fealty is that we are slaves to what we worship, the Law of Freedom is this: the paradoxical reality that the greater the submission to Christ, the greater the freedom we will experience. The kingdom of God does turn "the world upside down" (Acts 17:6)... or is it right side up?

Redemption for a Reason

Paired with proclamations of our new-found freedom are many cautionary words. Peter instructs, "As God's slaves, live as free people, but don't use your freedom as a way to conceal evil (1 Peter 2:16). Paul writes, "Christ has liberated us to be free. Stand firm then and don't submit again to a yoke of slavery" and exhorts us to not "use this freedom as an opportunity for the flesh, but serve one another through love" (Galatians 5:1, 13).

How do we resist misusing our freedom or become enslaved again to sin? I submit three strategies: Sabbath, gratitude, and good works.

Sabbath has been woven into the rhythms of creation since God rested on that very first seventh day. But, it was not a command[67] until the Ten Commandments were delivered at Mount Sinai. This came after 400 years of the Israelites suffering under brutal Egyptian captivity, where "they worked the Israelites ruthlessly and made their lives bitter with difficult labor" (Exodus 1:13–14). Week after week, for centuries, the Israelites did not experience a Sabbath rest.

The word *Sabbath* is derived from a Hebrew verb meaning to stop, cease, or rest. It is a day to stop keeping our "nose to the grindstone"; to cease all strivings; to rest in the faithful love and

---

67   The Sabbath was instituted along with the provision of manna (Exodus 16:21–23) and then etched onto the Ten Commandments (the fourth commandment, to be exact. See Exodus 20:8–11). Here we see another paradox—that God would have to command us to do something designed for our benefit and enjoyment.

provision of the Lord. It is a declaration that we are not slaves to the world or our work. And a reminder that, when we pause, the sun still rises with no help on our part. Sabbath brings perspective and reminds us of whom we serve. Sabbath shouts, "Freedom!"

If pride is the subversively snaking essence of all sin, then gratitude is the antivenom. Gratitude protects us from forgetting who really sits on the throne in our lives and provides every breath we take. It protects us from holier-than-thou judgment because we realize that "we too were once foolish, disobedient, deceived, enslaved by various passions and pleasures" (Titus 3:3). Therefore, we practice gratitude for our freedom rather than diagnosing faults in others.

Gratitude protects us from fear. Jesus has freed us, we "who were held in slavery all their lives by the fear of death" (Hebrews 2:15). "For you did not receive a spirit of slavery to fall back into fear, but you received the Spirit of adoption, by whom we cry out, 'Abba, Father!'" (Romans 8:15). And when we worry and fear, we are to cry out to our Father "through prayer and petition *with thanksgiving*" (Philippians 4:6). This is how we obtain "the peace of God, which surpasses every thought" which "will guard your hearts and minds in Christ Jesus" (Philippians 4:7). Gratitude defends us against falling back into slavery.

Thirdly, practicing "good works" helps us live rightly in our freedom. Rather than selfishly serving ourselves, we are to serve others. Paul explained it this way: "Although I am a free man and not anyone's slave, I have made myself a slave to everyone, in order to win more people" (1 Corinthians 9:19). Paul says he does this all for the gospel: "I have become all things to all people, so that I may by every possible means save some" (1 Corinthians 9:22).

Though the gospel is offensive to the world and human pride, we are to always share truth in love:

> The Lord's slave must not quarrel, but must be gentle to everyone, able to teach, and patient, instructing his opponents with gentleness. Perhaps God will grant them repentance leading them to the knowledge of the truth. Then they may come to their senses and escape the Dev-

il's trap, having been captured by him to do his will.
(2 Timothy 2:24–26)

Christians are freedom fighters sent in love to proclaim the good news to those still held captive.

Of course, we are to exercise good works within the church—to build up the Body and as a picture of Christlike love to the world. We can "wash one another's feet" by bearing each other's burdens, utilizing our spiritual giftings, and outdoing one another in showing love. The fight to live out our freedom takes teamwork.

Abiding in our freedom also requires endurance. To reference James again, "The one who looks intently into the perfect law of freedom and *perseveres* in it. . .this person will be blessed in what he does" (James 1:25). But, be encouraged! Battles may rage now, but we know the war is already won.

Jesus has conquered sin and death and set us free and "if the Son sets you free, you really will be free" (John 8:36). So, in this age where we wait for His return, we set our hope on our heavenly, perfect, and final freedom. Even creation expectantly looks forward to that day:

> For I consider that the sufferings of this present time are not worth comparing with the glory that is going to be revealed to us. For the creation eagerly waits with anticipation for God's sons to be revealed. For the creation was subjected to futility—not willingly, but because of Him who subjected it—in the hope that the creation itself will also be set free from the bondage of corruption into the glorious freedom of God's children.
> (Romans 8:18–21)

So we stay "ready for service and have our lamps lit" awaiting the return of Christ, our Master (Luke 12:35). He will bring that future revelation of glory unimaginably great—where all chains of this sinful world are forgotten and our freedom is complete, a divine and supreme Sabbath rest. This will be a reality ruled by the Law of Freedom, where we will serve our King, and He, in turn, serves us with His bountiful and rich grace.

Free at last
He has ransomed me
His grace runs deep
While I was a slave to sin
Jesus died for me
Yes He died for me
Who the Son sets free
Oh is free indeed [68]

---

68   "Who You Say I Am" by Hillsong Worship.

7

What's in a Name?

How sweet the name of Jesus sounds
in a believer's ear!
It soothes our sorrows, heals our wounds,
and drives away our fear.

John Newton, 1779

Only one name has the power to save us.
(Eternal One, You stand alone.)
Only one name has the strength to heal.
(Exalted King upon the throne)
Only one name causes demons to tremble.
(Eternal One, You stand alone.)
Only one name sets the captives free.
(Exalted King)

***For Today, "The Only Name"*[69]**

---

69 "The Only Name." *Immortal*, by For Today. Razor & Tie Records, 2012.

The year was 2000 and the California Prune Board decided it was time for a rebrand. In an effort to market to a younger audience, they changed their name to the California Dried Plum Board. What was behind the identity crisis? The perception was that prunes were only found in grandma's refrigerator and only eaten when one needed to. . .well. . ."get things moving"—digestively, that is. The board stuck with the name for nearly twenty years until "prunes" became an in-vogue health food and they again adjusted to the market, reverting to their former name.

When humans want to change how others view—how they identify—something or someone, we name (or rename) it.

Power to Name

The ability to assign a name implies authority. Parents name children. Entrepreneurs name their company and product creations. Scientists who have discovered new animals or stars are often granted the privilege of naming them (hence, we end up with names such as "lightbulb anemone" or "Herbig-Haro 211").

The first time we see the assignment of names in Scripture is in the fifth verse of the Bible: "God called the light 'day,' and He called the darkness 'night.' Evening came and then morning: the first day" (Genesis 1:5). As God continues to craft all creation, He also names the sky, earth, and seas (vv. 8–10). Why does the Bible tell us that God *named* each of these parts of creation? Why not simply say He made them? I would suggest that it emphasizes His authority—His lordship. The Lord is King over everything "in heaven and on earth and under the earth" (Philippians 2:10). He is the "Ancient of Days"—Lord over time itself.

We then find something remarkable. God does not name all of the creatures He speaks forth on the fifth and sixth days of creation. Instead, He hands over this authority to Adam. The Lord brings each animal to the man "to see what he would call it. And whatever the man called a living creature, that was its name" (Genesis 2:19).

Naming reflects both our God-gifted authority and creativity. It is, in part, how we "fill the earth and subdue it" (Genesis 1:28). We utilize the raw material God has provided to create which then comes with new language for those creations.

In the process of naming the animals, Adam realizes he does not have a suitable counterpart (presumably, in part, due to each species of animal having a male and female version). So, God performs the first anesthesia and surgery, and handcrafts the man's complement. God brings her to Adam and he exclaims:

> This one, at last, is bone of my bone
> and flesh of my flesh;
> this one will be called "woman,"
> for she was taken from man.
> (Genesis 2:23)[70]

The first woman is not given the name "Eve" until after the world falls under the curse (see Genesis 3:20). The sting of death would now be felt by all humanity, and yet Adam chooses to name his wife Eve, which means "life" or "living." Eve would be the "mother of all the living," and in her name we hear echoes of faith, and the hope of redemption.

So, we see that names are more than a way of distinguishing people, places, and things. Names carry meaning. Names speak of identity.

Making a Name

Story of our Lives

Names communicate meaning, and behind that meaning is usually a story.

Moses sounds like "drawing out" in Hebrew and he was drawn out of the water (Exodus 2:10). He would be God's chosen instrument to draw the Israelites out of Egypt. As the Israelites are wandering in the wilderness, they name locations such as Marah, Massah, and Meribah. Which mean "bitterness," "testing," and "arguing," respectively (see Exodus 15:23, 17:7). All fitting names during this forty-year period. When God promises hundred-year-

---

70   The naming shows the "headship" of the man; however, Adam's choice of language also speaks to their divine Image-bearing equality. Then there's the old joke that the name represents what Adam said when he saw her: "Whoa, man!"

old Abraham and ninety-year-old Sarah that they will have a son, they both laugh and the son is given the name Isaac, meaning "he laughs" (see Genesis 17:15–18:15).[71]

There are hundreds of examples throughout the Bible of the "why" behind the names of people and places. It is also important to pay attention to when a name changes. One of the reasons a name will change is due to a life-changing incident: an encounter with the Living God.

In Genesis 17, God appears to Abram and richly reiterates His covenant promises. The Lord then gives new names to Abram and Sarai. They become Abaraham, "Father of a Multitude," and Sarah, meaning "Princess" (vv. 5, 15). Every day, they would speak these new names and be reminded that the Lord rules over their lives and He keeps His promises.

Abraham's grandson would also experience a divine renaming. One night, a "man" wrestles with Jacob until daybreak. Jacob refuses to give up unless the nameless man blesses him first.

> "What is your name?" the man asked.
> "Jacob," he replied.
> "Your name will no longer be Jacob," He said. "It will be Israel because you have struggled with God and with men and have prevailed."
> Then Jacob asked Him, "Please tell me Your name."
> But He answered, "Why do you ask My name?" And He blessed him there.
> Jacob then named the place Peniel, "For I have seen God face to face," he said, "and I have been delivered."
> (Genesis 32:27–30)

The name *Israel* in Hebrew sounds like "one who wrestles or struggles with God." It's a fitting name, both for Jacob and the nation that would come through him. The newly renamed patriarch then renames the location as Peniel, literally "the face of God." Everything changes when God shows up.

Turning to the New Testament, let us observe one more example. Jesus asks His disciples who they believe He is. Simon

---

71   I interpret this as God having an excellent sense of holy sarcasm.

responds, calling Jesus the "Messiah, the Son of the living God" (Matthew 16:16). Jesus answers him, "Simon son of Jonah, you are blessed because flesh and blood did not reveal this to you, but My Father in heaven. And I also say to you that you are Peter, and on this rock I will build My church" (vv. 17–18). Again, we find: a divine encounter, the delivery of God's promises, and a new, distinctive name granted to the one whom the Lord will use to carry out His promises.

These examples show the Lord's authority, creativity, and how He graciously includes us in His mysterious and redemptive plans. While humans imitate these qualities, sadly, we also abuse this God-gifted authority.

Babel-ing Fools

Eight chapters after the fall, we come to the story of the Tower of Babylon. The people share one language and are one in their objective:

> And they said, "Come, let us build ourselves a city and a tower with its top in the sky. Let us make a name for ourselves; otherwise, we will be scattered over the face of the whole earth."

> Then the LORD came down to look over the city and the tower that the men were building. The LORD said, "If they have begun to do this as one people all having the same language, then nothing they plan to do will be impossible for them. Come, let Us go down there and confuse their language so that they will not understand one another's speech." So from there the LORD scattered them over the face of the whole earth, and they stopped building the city. Therefore its name is called Babylon.
> (Genesis 11:4–9)

There is more going on here than an explanation for the origin of multiple languages. It is a rebellion, a coup, a desire to usurp divine authority. To avoid being scattered over the earth is in direct opposition to God's command to "be fruitful and multiply" and "spread out over the earth" (originally Genesis 1:28 and then repeated to Noah and his family after the flood. See Genesis 9:7). To build a tower into the heavens exhibits their godlike aspirations. And to "make a name" for themselves is to say that their gifted authority is not enough. They want more. They want to be the sole authority defining themselves and reality.

It is the same sinful pride seen in the garden—a corrupt craving to eat from the tree of the knowledge of good and evil and become like God. In our selfish ambition, we look to idols to "enhance" our identity. We seek power and influence rather than the One whose "name is great in power" (Jeremiah 10:6). We strive after riches and wealth instead of the One who is rich in faithful love. We chase after making our name famous rather than pursuing a relationship with the Famous One.

But humanity's renaming does not stop there. We ate from the tree of the knowledge of good and evil and now attempt to redefine reality by twisting that knowledge around. We give our own meanings to words or concepts such as love, freedom, or truth. Atrocious genocide becomes "ethnic cleansing." Heinous murder becomes "my body, my choice." Failure to rejoice and agree with those who parade their sins is deemed "hateful" and "bigotry." Declaring biblical truth receives illogical *ad hominem* attacks. Men can be women. Women can be men. "My truth" trumps all—and who is God to say otherwise?

"Woe to those who call evil good and good evil," writes Isaiah (Isaiah 5:20). When we selfishly manipulate God's good namings, we end up in an identity crisis. With fluid self-defined terminology, we are just babbling fools.

"If you are. . ."

As if our own sinful inclinations were not enough, our enemies use naming to exert control and influence our identity.

Israel's history gives us a glimpse into this strategy. Due to their wickedness, the Lord hands over Israel to the conquering Babylonians. Among those captured and put into service in Babylon were Daniel, Hananiah, Mishael, and Azariah. One of the first actions the

Bible highlights is that the chief Babylonian official renames these young men. This was so effective that even most modern Christians know the last three better by their pagan names: Shadrach, Meshach, and Abednego. Daniel was renamed Belteshazzar. Names that honored the true and living God were replaced with names praising false gods. (For example: Mishael or "Who Is What God Is?" became Meshach or "Who Is What Aku Is?")

The Babylonians also deported the king at that time, Jehoiachin. "Then the king of Babylon made Mattaniah, Jehoiachin's uncle, king in his place and changed his name to Zedekiah" (2 Kings 24:17). The message is clear: "We are now your authority—forget who you are and your God."

Our spiritual foe, Satan, employs the same strategy. He tempts us with the "lust of the flesh, the lust of the eyes, and the pride in one's lifestyle" (1 John 2:16), all the while questioning God's truthful Word and who God says we are. It is spiritual identity theft.

The inauguration of Jesus' earthly ministry is marked by His baptism. John the Baptist baptizes Jesus in the Jordan and:

> After Jesus was baptized, He went up immediately from the water. The heavens suddenly opened for Him, and He saw the Spirit of God descending like a dove and coming down on Him. And there came a voice from heaven:

> This is My beloved Son.
> I take delight in Him!
> (Matthew 3:16–17)

It's an incredible scene: The Triune Godhead in concert with glory and power as defining approval and identity are declared over Jesus.

And the very next verse in Matthew is: "Then Jesus was led up by the Spirit into the wilderness to be tempted by the Devil" (Matthew 4:1).

And what are the first words out of the devil's mouth?

> "If you are the Son of God. . ."
> (Matthew 4:3)

Satan slyly questions the identifying proclamation God has just made. He attacks Jesus' name while offering three temptations. It reeks of the same scheme used with similar venomous words, "Did God really say. . .?" (Genesis 3:1).

Pastor and author John Mark Comer does an excellent job illustrating the parallels here between the garden of Eden and the tempting of Jesus:

"The lust of the flesh" = "good for food" = stones to bread

"The lust of the eyes" = "pleasing to the eye" = the kingdoms and their splendor

"The pride of life" = "desirable for gaining wisdom" = the temple spectacle[72]

While the first Adam failed, the Second Adam remained sinless through His testing. Jesus leaned into the identity declared over Him and relied on the Word of God. By quoting Scripture, Jesus is answering the question, "Did God really say. . .?" with "Yes! He really did!"

While the French philosopher Descartes' famous "I think, therefore I am" deals with existence, that same thinking ability leads humans to other timeless existential questions. "Who am I?" "Why was I placed into this specific time and space?" "What is my purpose?" These are a few of the enduring questions humans have asked themselves.

What, or Who, informs the answers to these questions inevitably shapes our identity. Where do we derive the "names" for the things in our lives—for ourselves? From the world? The enemy? Our own pride?

Only a relationship with our Creator can solve our identity crisis.

The answer to our "Who am I?" is found in the great "I AM!"

---

72 John Mark Comer, *Live No Lies: Recognize and Resist the Three Enemies That Sabotage Your Peace* (Waterbrook, 2021). Additional parallels can be made between Jesus' forty-day testing in the wilderness and Israel's forty years in the wilderness and the tests they faced. This is a recommended exploration!

In The Name

I AM

The different names of God in the Bible each reveal different aspects of His character and how He relates to us.

The first name for God we encounter is *Elohim*, meaning simply "God" or "Creator." This name appears over two thousand times in the Old Testament. *Adonai* is another common name, meaning "Lord."

El Shaddai, which translates "Lord God Almighty," occurs seven times in the Old Testament. There is a strong connection between this name and God's covenantal promises to Abraham, Isaac, and Jacob (examples include: Genesis 17:1, 28:3, 35:11). The promises of God are always underwritten by His sovereign might and good Name. He never has—and never will—fail to fulfill His word.

There is one name used more than any other name for God in the Bible—Yahweh. This is the personal name for God, revealed first to Moses at the burning bush:

> Then Moses asked God, "If I go to the Israelites and say to them: The God of your fathers has sent me to you, and they ask me, 'What is His name?' what should I tell them?"

> God replied to Moses, "I AM WHO I AM. This is what you are to say to the Israelites: I AM has sent me to you." God also said to Moses, "Say this to the Israelites: Yahweh, the God of your fathers, the God of Abraham, the God of Isaac, and the God of Jacob, has sent me to you. This is My name forever; this is how I am to be remembered in every generation. (Exodus 3:13–15)

This is a simple, yet wonderfully profound Name. The tense in Hebrew encompasses past, present, and future. Yahweh is the "the One who is, who was, and who is coming" (Revelation 1:4).[73] He is eternal—outside of time, outside of constraining definition, outside of our full comprehension.

---

73   Notice the order in that verse. Present tense is listed first.

In this name, we see His independent, unchangeable, self-sufficient nature. Possessing self-sufficiency, Yahweh is accordingly all-sufficient; all else finds its origin and its sustained being in Him. He defines Himself and, indeed, all of reality. And the reality is that Yahweh is the only living, one true God, whereas all false gods and idols are naught. The Lord declares: "There is no other God but Me, a righteous God and Savior; there is no one except Me" (Isaiah 45:21).

The majesty of His name is recurrent in Scripture. The psalmist writes:

> Let them praise Your great and awe-inspiring name. He
> is holy.
> (Psalm 99:3)

> My mouth will declare Yahweh's praise;
> let every living thing
> praise His holy name forever and ever.
> (Psalm 145:21)

His name is to be treated with reverence. The third of the Ten Commandments is: "Do not misuse the name of the LORD your God, because the LORD will not leave anyone unpunished who misuses His name (Exodus 20:7). This does not mean we are to avoid using the Lord's name;[74] rather, we are to use it with integrity. To associate God's name with words or actions inconsistent with the meanings of His great name is to be flippant toward His holiness, dishonest about His character, and essentially to disregard His existence. It is about Yahweh's reputation and honor.

We see what He says when Israel misrepresents Him:

---

74   In an effort to not even come close to breaking this commandment, the Jews stopped saying or writing the name of God (most scholars believe this started around the time of the Babylonian exile). While not wanting to disrespect God's name is a good thing, I would argue that failing to say His name in connection to prayer, praise, and thanksgiving is itself a form of disrespect and goes against Scripture (a few examples include Deuteronomy 32:3, Psalm 29:2, Isaiah 12:4, and Amos 9:12). As with the hypocritical Pharisees of Jesus' day, the message of grace and relationship with Yahweh is displaced by myopic, meticulous adherence to misinterpreted Law.

"Therefore, say to the house of Israel: This is what the Lord GOD says: It is not for your sake that I will act, house of Israel, but for My holy name, which you profaned among the nations where you went. I will honor the holiness of My great name, which has been profaned among the nations—the name you have profaned among them. The nations will know that I am Yahweh"—the declaration of the Lord GOD—"when I demonstrate My holiness through you in their sight."
(Ezekiel 36:22–23)

As Jesus started the prayer He taught the disciples: "Our Father in heaven, Your name be honored as holy" (Matthew 6:9).

For all of His loftiness, holiness, and mystery, Yahweh is not a remote, uncaring, aloof God. No, He makes Himself known to us. Yahweh is near and ever present. His desire is that people know Him. Yahweh's promises of salvation are for all peoples and nations. Even when Israel disobeyed, God told them: "I have let you live for this purpose: to show you My power and to make My name known in all the earth" (Exodus 9:16). He cares deeply for all people. And, in His sovereignty, He weaves together all events for our good (Romans 8:28).

When Yahweh does define Himself, what does He say? We find out when He displays His glory to Moses:

The LORD came down in a cloud, stood with him there, and proclaimed His name Yahweh. Then the LORD passed in front of him and proclaimed:

Yahweh—Yahweh is a compassionate and gracious God, slow to anger and rich in faithful love and truth
(Exodus 34:5–6)

That the Lord even partially grants Moses' request to see His glory (Exodus 33:18) is amazing and speaks to His character. Even more amazing is the language with which He reveals deeper definitions to His name.

He reveals His name to us, and also knows each of us by

name! Just before Moses' request in Exodus 33, what does God say? "You have found favor in My sight, and I know you by name" (v. 17). This, of course, does not only apply to Moses. For these words from the Lord are for all believers: "Do not fear, for I have redeemed you; I have called you by your name; you are Mine" (Isaiah 43:1). "He calls his own sheep by name" (John 10:3).

Yahweh, the Lord of all creation, knows you—and me—by name! In the words of Dale Carnegie, "A person's name is, to that person, the sweetest and most important sound in any language."[75] Can you imagine Yahweh saying your name?

Though He exists outside of time, Yahweh chooses to step into time and space to be with us. Although He is omnipresent and always "with" us, there is no better representation of this than in the wonderful name "Immanuel."

Isaiah recorded the prophecy that, "the Lord Himself will give you a sign: The virgin will conceive, have a son, and name him Immanuel (Isaiah 7:14). Over 700 years later, the angel Gabriel would announce to Mary:

> Do not be afraid, Mary,
> for you have found favor with God.
> Now listen:
> You will conceive and give birth to a son,
> and you will call His name Jesus.
> He will be great
> and will be called the Son of the Most High,
> and the Lord God will give Him
> the throne of His father David.
> He will reign over the house of Jacob forever,
> and His kingdom will have no end.

> Mary asked the angel, "How can this be, since I have not been intimate with a man?"

> The angel replied to her:

75　Dale Carnegie, *How to Win Friends and Influence People* (New York, Simon & Schuster: 1936; rev. ed., 1981), 47.

> "The Holy Spirit will come upon you,
> and the power of the Most High will overshadow you.
> Therefore, the holy One to be born
> will be called the Son of God.
> (Luke 1:30–35)

The Father, Son, and Holy Spirit in spectacular concert as the great I AM becomes human to dwell among us. The incredible incarnation—the Word became flesh (John 1:14). God, eternal and mighty, "emptied Himself . . . taking on the likeness of men" (Philippians 2:7). God with us (Immanuel) to "save His people from their sins" (Matthew 1:21). Remember, the name Jesus (Yeshua), means "Yahweh saves."

Jesus is the manifestation of what Yahweh proclaimed to Moses.

As He traveled and taught, He was filled with compassion for the people "because they were weary and worn out, like sheep without a shepherd" (Matthew 9:36). Jesus is the essence and vessel of the graciousness of God. "We have redemption in Him through His blood, the forgiveness of our trespasses, according to the riches of His grace" (Ephesians 1:7). Jesus displayed an almost incomprehensible slowness to anger—even while in agony on the cross: "Father, forgive them, because they do not know what they are doing" (Luke 23:34).

And Jesus flawlessly melded love and truth in His interactions with others. He lovingly handled the situation with the woman caught in adultery by the Pharisees but also told her, "Go, and from now on do not sin anymore" (John 8:11).

In Christ Jesus, we find the marriage of the Lord's mercy and justice; the reconciliation of His wrath and love. As MacLaren describes it in his expositions:

> Jesus has borne the burden of sin and the weight of the divine Justice. The lips that said "Be of good cheer, thy sins be forgiven thee," also cried, "Why hast Thou forsaken Me?" The tenderest manifestation of the God "plenteous in mercy . . . forgiving iniquity," and the most awe-kindling manifestation of the God "that will by no

means clear the guilty," are fused into one.[76]

All the attributes of the Almighty Glorious One are revealed through Christ Jesus (John 1:18). The one who has seen Him has seen the Father (John 14:9).

In the Old Testament, God's name is fused with descriptors of His character to form compound names. Here we find names such as:

Yahweh Yireh or Jehovah-Jireh—The Lord will Provide (Genesis 22:14)
Yahweh Nissi or Jehovah Nissi—The Lord is my Banner (Exodus 17:15)
Yahweh Rophe or Jehovah Rapha—The Lord Who Heals (Exodus 15:26)

Behind each of these names is a remarkable story demonstrating aspects of the Lord's nature.

Seven times in the Gospel of John, Jesus creates new compound names using "I AM" to teach and reveal more about Himself.

He proclaims, "I am. . .

1. The bread of life (John 6:25)
2. The light of the world (John 8:12)
3. The door (or gate) of the sheep (John 10:7)
4. The good shepherd (John 10:14)
5. The resurrection and the life (John 11:25)
6. The way, the truth, and the life (John 14:6)
7. The true vine (John 15:5)

Much can be said about each of these titles, but our aim here is to simply make the Old and New Testament connection of the compound names of Yahweh.

John continues this theme in his writing. When Judas and his band of miscreants arrived to arrest Jesus,

---

[76] https://biblehub.com/library/maclaren/expositions_of_holy_scripture_k/
god_proclaiming_his_own_name.htm

"Jesus, knowing everything that was about to happen to
Him, went out and said to them, "Who is it you're looking
for?"

"Jesus the Nazarene," they answered.

"I am He," Jesus told them.

Judas, who betrayed Him, was also standing with them.
When He told them, "I am He," they stepped back and fell
to the ground.
(John 18:4–6)

This group of armed soldiers and temple police were there to
seize Jesus, yet they find themselves seized by some strange stu-
pefied awe upon hearing the words "I am."

In an earlier incident (recorded in John 8:56–58), Jesus was
teaching in the temple and told the crowd:

Your father Abraham was overjoyed that he would see My
day; he saw it and rejoiced."

The Jews replied, "You aren't 50 years old yet, and You've
seen Abraham?"

Jesus said to them, "I assure you: Before Abraham was,
I am."

At that, they picked up stones to throw at Him. But Jesus
was hidden and went out of the temple complex.

There is no ambiguity as to why the Jews wanted to immediately enact the death penalty on Jesus. Make no mistake, in all of
His uses of this name, Jesus is clearly claiming to be Yahweh.

What name would you ascribe to Jesus? A decent teacher? A
prophet? One of many ways to heaven?

C.S. Lewis brilliantly comments on this quandary in the timeless book, *Mere Christianity*:

A man who was merely a man and said the sort of things Jesus said would not be a great moral teacher. He would either be a lunatic—on the level with the man who says he is a poached egg—or else he would be the Devil of Hell. You must make your choice. Either this man was, and is, the Son of God, or else a madman or something worse. You can shut him up for a fool, you can spit at him and kill him as a demon or you can fall at his feet and call him Lord and God, but let us not come with any patronizing nonsense about his being a great human teacher. He has not left that open to us. He did not intend to.[77]

If Jesus is the Lord God—and He is—then it changes everything. We now turn to look at the impact this has on us personally.
There is power in the name of Jesus!

In Jesus' Name

During the earliest days of the church, the gospel was miraculously and powerfully spreading to all peoples, nations, and tongues. Some vagabond Jewish exorcists—the seven sons of the high priest, Sceva—took notice of this. They decided they would attempt to "pronounce the name of the Lord Jesus over those who had evil spirits, saying, 'I command you by the Jesus that Paul preaches!'"(Acts 19:13). The results were not quite what they expected:

> The evil spirit answered them, "I know Jesus, and I recognize Paul—but who are you?" Then the man who had the evil spirit leaped on them, overpowered them all, and prevailed against them, so that they ran out of that house naked and wounded. This became known to everyone who lived in Ephesus, both Jews and Greeks. Then fear fell on all of them, and the name of the Lord Jesus was magnified. (Acts 19:15–17)

77 C. S. Lewis, 2012. *Mere Christianity.* C. S. Lewis Signature Classic. London, England: William Collins, 32.

The name of Jesus is nothing to trifle with. It is not a magic word, cheap trick, or formula to be used for selfish gain. Ironically, the sons of Sceva misusing the name of Jesus led to His name being venerated all the more.

As we shall see, there are proper and powerful occasions in which the name of Jesus is used in Scripture.

In the book of Acts, there are many references to preaching in the name of Jesus (Acts 4:18, 8:12, 9:27, to name a few). In fact, the apostles and early disciples were so effective in this preaching that more than once they were threatened by the Sanhedrin and ordered "not to preach or teach at all in the name of Jesus (Acts 4:18). But intimidation tactics and even flogging could not halt the spread of the gospel, and the disciples rejoiced "that they were counted worthy to be dishonored on behalf of the Name" (Acts 5:41).

In addition to preaching, miracles are recorded as being done "in the name of Jesus." The early Christians prayed, "Grant that Your slaves may speak Your message with complete boldness, while You stretch out Your hand for healing, signs, and wonders to be performed through the name of Your holy Servant Jesus" (Acts 4:29–30).

When Peter passed by a man who was born lame sitting next to the temple gate, he said to him, "I don't have silver or gold, but what I have, I give you: In the name of Jesus Christ the Nazarene, get up and walk!" (Acts 3:6). The man "jumped up, stood, and started to walk, and he entered the temple complex with them— walking, leaping, and praising God" (v. 8).

In Philippi, a slave girl started following Paul, Luke, and their companions. She was oppressed by a "spirit of prediction" and turned a "large profit for her owners by fortune-telling" (Acts 16:16). For days, she followed them and called out, "These men, who are proclaiming to you the way of salvation, are the slaves of the Most High God" (Acts 16:17; the demon was not wrong!). Paul said to the evil spirit, "'I command you in the name of Jesus Christ to come out of her!' And it came out right away" (v. 18).

Why emphasize all of these things as being "in Jesus' name"? Why not just say they performed miracles, preached, and taught? Why do believers end prayers that way? Why baptize in the name of the Father, Son, and Holy Spirit?

Because, "There is salvation in no one else, for there is no other name under heaven given to people, and we must be saved by it" (Acts 4:12). Jesus is the one and only Messiah. As Paul rhetorically asks the Corinthian church: "Were you baptized in Paul's name?" (1 Corinthians 1:13). He is the One due all honor and glory and we proclaim His name in order that others "may believe Jesus is the Messiah, the Son of God, and by believing you may have life in His name" (John 20:31).

Through the Holy Spirit, His power works through us and whatever we do "in word or in deed, [we] do everything in the name of the Lord Jesus, giving thanks to God the Father through Him" (Colossians 3:17). We proclaim Jesus and, by doing so, identify with Him.

When we are saved through Jesus, we experience an extraordinary transformation. Paul writes in his letter to the church at Colossae, "For you have died, and your life is hidden with the Messiah in God" (Colossians 3:3). All believers can say, "I have been crucified with Christ and I no longer live, but Christ lives in me. The life I now live in the body, I live by faith in the Son of God, who loved me and gave Himself for me" (Galatians 2:19–20). Whereas Satan attempts spiritual identity theft, Christ Jesus brings identity thriving.

Now, this is not to say that we "lose ourselves" in the process. This is not some form of asceticism where all aspects of the physical are evil. No, each one of us is uniquely handcrafted by God and has "been remarkably and wonderfully made" (Psalm 139:14).

Like a bride takes on the groom's family name, the church—the bride of Christ—"puts on" Christ and becomes united with her loving Savior. His priorities become our priorities. Every aspect of our lives—thought, word, and deed—undergoes tuning that we may be useful instruments to Yahweh.

The fancy theological name for this process is sanctification. And it is not instantaneous; it is a process. This is not replacement, but renewal. We are becoming more of who we are meant to be.

So, how does one transform our identity and take off the "old self" and put on the "new self"? An entire book could be written on this; however, I would submit there are two aspects. One, by putting the "old ways" to death—and not just to death, but crucifying them. Secondly, living in new ways—that is, in Christ.

In Paul's letters, he constantly writes about these "negative" and "positive" aspects of sanctification. Do not participate with the darkness, but walk in the light (Ephesians 5:6–14). Do not be "conformed" to this world, instead be "transformed" (Romans 12:2). Like a battery, we need both the positive and the negative to realize the full power of sanctification.

Notice the repetitive theme of *renewal*, especially of one's mind. We are "being renewed in knowledge according to the image of [our] Creator," being "transformed by the renewing of [our] mind," and are being renewed in the spirit of [our] minds" (Colossians 3:10; Romans 12:2; Ephesians 4:23, respectively).

This makes sense, does it not? For our thoughts give birth to speech and actions. Modern research into neuroplasticity shows that through focus, repetition, and conscientiousness we can literally rewire our brains and form new neural connections. Scientific discoveries now back up "taking every thought captive" (2 Corinthians 10:5) and to dwell on whatever is true, honorable, just, pure, lovely, and commendable (Philippians 4:8). Through renewing our minds, the power of the Holy Spirit, and the living and effective Word of God, we really can have the "mind of Christ" (1 Corinthians 2:16).

And believers now evaluate the world around them in a new way. The way we "name" things in life is different.

> We also speak these things, not in words taught by human wisdom, but in those taught by the Spirit, explaining spiritual things to spiritual people. But the unbeliever does not welcome what comes from God's Spirit, because it is foolishness to him; he is not able to understand it since it is evaluated spiritually. The spiritual person, however, can evaluate everything
> (1 Corinthians 2:13–15)

Our unveiled minds have a new way of seeing things. Trials and sufferings are now opportunities for refining faith and producing spiritual fruit. Believers understand that we are temporary residents and possess eternal perspective.

We are not defined by the insults or labels of others, nor by comparison to our neighbor. We are not defined by our sin and shortcomings, nor our wealth or accomplishments. We are not defined by flaming arrows from the evil one.

Believers are adopted sons and daughters of one spiritual family, co-heirs with Christ. We are more than conquerors. We are redeemed; gospel witnesses; worshippers in Spirit and truth; salt and light; God's coworkers; ambassadors for Christ. We are sheep under the care of the Good Shepherd. Jesus defines our identity and is in control of our story.

The renewal process does not end this side of eternity. But, "when the Messiah, who is your life, is revealed, then you also will be revealed with Him in glory" (Colossians 3:4). We are "to deny godlessness and worldly lusts and to live in a sensible, righteous, and godly way in the present age, while we wait for the blessed hope and appearing of the glory of our great God and Savior, Jesus Christ" (Titus 2:12–13). This is our blessed hope!

On that day, when Jesus returns in brilliant glory, His name will "be exalted above all blessing and praise" (Nehemiah 9:5).

> He humbled Himself by becoming obedient
> to the point of death—
> even to death on a cross.
> For this reason God highly exalted Him
> and gave Him the name
> that is above every name,
> so that at the name of Jesus
> every knee will bow—
> of those who are in heaven and on earth
> and under the earth—
> and every tongue should confess
> that Jesus Christ is Lord,
> to the glory of God the Father.
> (Philippians 2:8–11)

Jesus came as a humble baby, a suffering servant. But He will return as a warrior king. John describes this vision in Revelation:

> Then I saw heaven opened, and there was a white horse. Its rider is called Faithful and True, and He judges and makes war in righteousness. His eyes were like a fiery flame, and many crowns were on His head. He had a name written that no one knows except Himself. He wore a robe stained with blood, and His name is the Word of God. . . . And He has a name written on His robe and on His thigh:
>
> KING OF KINGS
> AND LORD OF LORDS.
> (19:11–13, 16)

The Word that became flesh and dwelt among us is coming again. He is faithful and never fails to keep His promises. His wrath is always righteous and truthful. With a robe still stained with the blood of the new covenant, Christ will execute the Lord's judgment and none shall stand against Him. Whether willingly or not—every knee will bow.

The doubly written names on His robe and thigh[78] show the emphasis His absolute authority—"far above every ruler and authority, power and dominion, and every title given, not only in this age but also in the one to come" (Ephesians 1:21). And though He has many fitting names—Wonderful Counselor, Prince of Peace, Immanuel, Lamb of God, Horn of Salvation—there is a name no one knows except He Himself—that is, which no other being can fully comprehend as it is far too wonderful. Indeed, "the hidden things belong to the Lord our God" and "all the treasures of wisdom and knowledge are hidden in Him" (Deuteronomy 29:29; Colossians 2:3).

So we join the chorus of the "song of the Lamb":

> Great and awe-inspiring are Your works,

---

78   Commentators generally believe this name is on the part of the robe covering the thigh or on a sword fastened at the thigh. I would humbly submit the view that it is actually written on His thigh, thus symbolizing: 1) His great promises and blessings, just as Abraham and Jacob had others place a hand under their thigh to pronounce oaths, and 2) That, as the ultimate sacrifice, Jesus was the "thigh of the contribution that is lifted up" (Exodus 29:27) and He is our portion.

Lord God, the Almighty;
righteous and true are Your ways,
King of the Nations.
Lord, who will not fear
and glorify Your name?
(Revelation 15:3–4)

The power of God's name is so great that Scripture speaks of where His name dwells. This is a place of His choosing (Deuteronomy 12:5; Ezra 6:12; Jeremiah 7:12). Under the Old Covenant, this was wherever the Ark of the Covenant was—the ark "called by the Name, the name of Yahweh of Hosts who dwells between the cherubim" (2 Samuel 6:2).[79]

But in the New Jerusalem, there is no sanctuary (Revelation 21:22). So, where does God choose to have His name dwell? The answer is this: All believers will bear His name! Jesus, the One whose name is above all names, tells His followers "I will never erase [your] name from the book of life but will acknowledge [your] name before My Father and before His angels" (Revelation 3:5). What incomprehensibly beautiful words those will be to hear!

Not only that, but Christ says, "I will write on him the name of My God and the name of the city of My God—the new Jerusalem, which comes down out of heaven from My God—and My new name" (3:12). Like the 144,000, His name will dwell with each of us! (14:1).

Then, together, we shall joyously thrive in our fully redeemed identities, a people for His possession, with the praises of His Name ever on our lips.

---

79   This is the Shekinah glory.

8

Fractals & Echoes

Mathematics is the language in which God has written the universe.

Galileo Galilei

Time is given us to use in view of eternity.

Harry Ironside

Math was discovered by humans, not invented.

In the beginning, God spoke the universe into being. In those words were colors and constellations, beaches and black holes, elements and energy, quasars and quarks. But, this was not a chaotic and confusing creation. There was a method to the madness: numbers.

In the creativity of God, beauty is melded with logic, and there is an intricate elegance to the numerical patterns in nature.

For instance, there is just a handful of fundamental constants underlying much of what governs the functions in our universe. The speed of light, Planck's constant, Avogadro's number, and the elementary charge (often simply referred to as "e") are but a few examples.

Several of the constants seen in nature are irrational—meaning they go on forever after the decimal place and never repeat. The irrational constants you probably learned about in grade school, pi and e have even been proven to be transcendental numbers (yes, that is a real mathematical term). Could it be that these ubiquitous incalculable constants point to an infinite Creator?[80]

The ways in which these numbers, discovered in different times in history and within different disciplines of math, interrelate is simply dumbfounding. Euler's equation depicts this perfectly. It is expressed as: $e{\wedge}i\pi + 1 = 0$.

> Euler's Formula encapsulates the whole of existence. It contains 0, the number of the monad (ontological zero); the number e that determines exponentiation; the number i that determines the imaginary domain (time); the number 1 that determines the domain of counting numbers (and with 0 creates the binary system of computing), and real numbers (space); -1, the number of the negative domain (antimatter); and the number π that determines the world of the circle and geometry. Euler's Formula is the unquestionable God Equation.[81]

---

80   Our ability to even discover and calculate such mathematics, to me, seems a miracle. To view a mind-blowing example of all the precise variables necessary for life on earth (a probability which exceeds the known universe, by the way) visit: https://reasons.org/explore/publications/articles/probability-for-life-on-earth.

81   Mike Hockney, *The God Equation* (Kindle Edition: Hyperreality Books, 2012).

One final example we must turn our attention to is fractals. These are repeating "patterns within a pattern." Looking at a leaf, lightning bolt, or our own circulatory system, these patterns will become evident. Take a tree and look at the largest offshoot or the smallest branch. Both look like smaller versions of the whole tree. As Benoit Mandelbrot, the mathematician known as the "father of fractals" said, "A fractal is a way of seeing infinity."

Without the discovery of these essential numbers and equations, none of our modern technology would exist. Computers, radio, satellites, chemistry, quantum physics, artificial intelligence, electricity, financial markets, and all fields of engineering utilize these principles. Discovering and implementing the mathematical constants and concepts of our universe is part of how humans carry out our Genesis 1 mandate to fill the earth and subdue it.

The point is these figures and equations are uncannily woven into the workings of the universe and speak to God's sovereignty and creativity—creativity that He designed in such a way that we can also discover and (at least for those who are mathematically inclined) understand these astounding numbers and concepts. While these numbers (like pi, e, phi, and C) aren't verbatim in Scripture, they are still "there" in the fact that they are in the mathematical DNA of creation itself. But, speaking of Scripture, we now turn to thematically significant numbers in the Bible.

Zero In

Let us take a moment to place parameters around the rest of this chapter's adventure. One must be careful in the interpretation of numbers in Scripture. Sound rules of biblical exegesis still apply, and context is key. In this chapter, we are not attempting to decipher any eschatological dates or other future events. We are not applying any sort of numerology, mysticism, or Kabbalistic nonsense.[82]

For our purposes, the focus will be on a few specific important numbers. There are over 7,000 numbers referenced in the Old

---

82 Kabbalah is a form of Jewish mysticism that often deals with deciphering "secret" knowledge.

Testament alone.[83] Within those numbers, I would submit that not all of them should be considered archetypal in nature.

For example, Seth was 912 years old when he died. To the extent that all Scripture is God-breathed and God is sovereign over all the days of our lives, this number is important. It was certainly important to Seth, his family, and the community he impacted over his lifetime. However, in terms of symbolism throughout Scripture, this is the only time in the entire Bible that this number shows up. It would be a stretch to give it any "deeper" meanings.

While there are other numbers that could be considered as symbolic patterns in Scripture (1, 4, 11, 30, 10,000, etc.), this adventure shall predominantly focus on four numbers: three, seven, twelve, and forty. These numbers echo through the pages of Scripture in a way that cannot be construed as coincidence.

For each number, we shall briefly examine the generally accepted archetypal meanings—where they are found both in nature and humanity. Then, we will take a deeper dive into their biblical occurrences and how all of these meanings fit together.

3

Once upon a time. . . there was the number three.

Three archetypally represents balance, stability, emphasis, structure, and harmony.

Stories have a beginning, middle, and end. Fairy tales, in particular, seem to have the number three embedded in their nature (for example: Goldilocks and the Three Bears, The Three Little Piggies, or Three Blind Mice). There are countless (pun intended) other examples and, in fact, there is a name for this concept: "The Rule of Three."

There is a certain stability humans ascribe to the number three, and this plays out in the physical world. A stool with two legs will fall over. With four legs, it may wobble. But, with three legs, it will always be stable on a flat floor. Triangles are some of the most stable shapes. Hence, they are seen in the engineering of bridges and other structures.

On a much smaller scale, the number three shows up again.

---

83 https://www.desiringgod.org/articles/counting-with-god.

DNA relies on a triplet coding system to turn the complex information in genes into the thousands of amino acids which are the building blocks of every living thing on earth. Looking in even greater depth, we see atoms are made up of three stable subatomic particles: protons, neutrons, and electrons. Protons and neutrons are each made up of exactly three smaller particles called quarks. Three is built into the foundational building blocks of all matter and life as we know it.

There are three primary colors from which we derive others, our music is built on triads, and a GPS system requires three satellites to triangulate one's position. So, we see that this number is of great importance to the structures that make up our world. But, when looking at the number three in the context of the Bible, will we discover similar themes?

Threefold

One of the most common uses of threes in the Bible is emphatic repetition, where a word or action is repeated thrice to display its importance.

When the Lord called Samuel to be His chosen prophet, He said Samuel's name three times. Samuel thought Eli the priest, whom he was serving under in the temple, was the one calling him. It was not until the third call that "Eli understood that the LORD was calling the boy. He told Samuel, "Go and lie down. If He calls you, say, 'Speak, LORD, for Your servant is listening.'" (1 Samuel 3:8–9).

The apostle Paul pleaded with the Lord three times to remove the "thorn in the flesh" that plagued him. After crying out three times, he received his answer from God: "My grace is sufficient for you, for power is perfected in weakness" (2 Corinthians 12:8–9).

The life of Elijah is a prime example of emphasis through threes. During his "competition" with the prophets of Baal to see who could call down fire from heaven to consume a sacrifice, he instructs servants to pour water on his altar three times (1 Kings 18:22–39).[84] King Ahaziah successively sends three groups of fifty

---

84 There is an intersection here with other intriguing numbers. Each pour of water is done with four pots, equaling twelve total pours. He also builds his altar using 12 stones for the 12 tribes of Israel.

soldiers to Elijah before a prophecy is delivered from Elijah to Ahaziah (the unfortunate first two groups of soldiers were consumed by fire Elijah called down from heaven). And, at the end of Elijah's life, three times he instructs his successor, Elisha, to stay behind in three different cities. But, three times, Elisha responds the same way: "As the LORD lives and as you yourself live, I will not leave you" (see 2 Kings 2:1–6).

Again, we encounter this pattern in the life of Jesus—especially surrounding His death and resurrection. Three times, Jesus, deeply troubled, prays in the garden of Gethsemane the night of His betrayal. In contrast to His faithful focus, three times we see Him rouse the sleepy disciples who are unable to stay vigilant (Matthew 26:36–46). Earlier that same eventful night, Jesus predicts that Peter will deny Him three times before the rooster crows (Matthew 26:34). It is not until after the resurrection of Jesus that we witness the rich counter emphasis of the Lord's grace in the threefold restoration of Peter:

This was now the third time Jesus appeared to the disciples after He was raised from the dead.

When they had eaten breakfast, Jesus asked Simon Peter, "Simon, son of John, do you love Me more than these?"

"Yes, Lord," he said to Him, "You know that I love You."

"Feed My lambs," He told him.

A second time He asked him, "Simon, son of John, do you love Me?"

"Yes, Lord," he said to Him, "You know that I love You."

"Shepherd My sheep," He told him.

He asked him the third time, "Simon, son of John, do you love Me?"

> Peter was grieved that He asked him the third time, "Do you love Me?" He said, "Lord, You know everything! You know that I love You."
> "Feed My sheep," Jesus said.
> (John 21:14–17)

The final note on emphatic threes we shall make is that there is only one word in all of Scripture describing God that is repeated in a grouping of three: holy. There are many descriptors aptly used of God and His character, but there is a certain loftiness and reverential awe communicated in the words "holy, holy, holy" (see Isaiah 6:3 and Revelation 4:8).

Special Structure

As triangles and triads add stable structure to bridges and music, so we find the number three showing up in physical and supernatural structures in the Bible.

Both the transportable tabernacle and the temples[85] consisted of three main sections: the courtyard, the sanctuary (holy place), and the most holy place (or holy of holies) (see Exodus 26; 1 Kings 6).

The most mysterious "structure" in Scripture is the trinitarian nature of God. He is three-in-one: Father, Son, and Holy Spirit. Beautiful, harmonious, and mind-boggling. And this fits with our archetypal meanings of three, does it not?

As far as stability, He is the definition of reliability and permanence. The Lord is immovable and steadfast—the same yesterday, today, and forevermore. When all else fails, He never will.

He is three-in-one. He is the beginning, middle, and end all at the same time. Simultaneously, He is the One who is, who was, and who is to come; the Alpha and Omega; the great I AM! The "structure" He reveals about Himself adds emphasis to His perfect omnipresence, omnipotence, and omniscience.

---

85 Solomon's temple which was destroyed by the Babylonians about 586 BC and Herod's temple which was destroyed by the Romans in AD 70.

Time and Times

An uncanny number of events in the Bible transpire over three hours, three days, or in the third year. We will examine a small sampling of these occurrences.

Every third year, in the sabbatical year cycles (that is, the third and sixth years with the seventh being the sabbath year) a special tithe was to be given "to the Levite, the foreigner, the fatherless, and the widow, so that they may eat in your towns and be satisfied" (Deuteronomy 26:12).

A "third-year theme" is found in the book of Daniel as well. Daniel is deported to Babylon in "the third year of the reign of Jehoiakim king of Judah" (Daniel 1:1). He also receives visions from the Lord in "the third year of King Belshazzar's reign" and in "the third year of Cyrus king of Persia" (Daniel 8:1; 10:1).

The most common threefold period of time in the Bible is three days. Abraham traveled three days to the place where he would offer up Isaac as a sacrifice (Genesis 22:4). Any meat of a fellowship sacrifice given as a vow or freewill offering was to be eaten by the priest who presented it; however, any leftover by the third day was to be burned up (Leviticus 7:16–18). On the third day at Mount Sinai, the Lord appeared with clouds, thunder, lightning, and fire before the Israelites (Exodus 19). Esther and her fellow Jews fasted for three days before her petition before the king on behalf of her people (Esther 4:16).

The ninth plague the Lord brought against Egypt was darkness. For three days a darkness so thick it could be felt enveloped the Egyptians (Exodus 10:21–23). After Paul's bright encounter with Jesus on the road to Damascus, he was unable to see for three days (Acts 9:10).

Finally, as we have already begun to see, the number three surrounds Jesus' arrest, trial, crucifixion, and resurrection. As Jesus, bloodied and gasping for air, hung on that rugged cross, darkness came over the land for three hours (Matthew 27:45). Then, at three in the afternoon, He gave up His spirit.[86] But after

---

86   The ninth hour—or three in the afternoon—was the time of the afternoon sacrifice. As this was during Passover, a multitude of people would have been gathered in the temple. Thousands of lambs were being sacrificed at the exact time our Saviour, the Lamb of God, sacrificed Himself to defeat sin and death. See

three days Christ's buried body would have breath again! Just as Jesus had promised, as He had referenced Jonah in the belly of the great fish and also to rebuild the temple in three days, so He was resurrected on the third day (see Matthew 12:40; John 2:19). Now we have salvation through Him.

> He will revive us after two days, and on the third day He will raise us up so we can live in His presence.
> (Hosea 6:2)

Hallelujah!

Beware the Dividing Thirds

It is worth noting when things are divided into thirds in Scripture. Inverting the number three gives way to opposite meanings. Where there was stability, there is now chaos. Structure collapses, and harmony turns to discord.[87]

The prophet Ezekiel dramatizes the future siege and fall of Jerusalem as God instructs him to shave his hair and beard and divide up the hair. The Lord then instructs Ezekiel:

> You are to burn up a third of it in the city when the days of the siege have ended; you are to take a third and slash it with the sword all around the city; and you are to scatter a third to the wind, for I will draw a sword to chase after them. But you are to take a few strands from the hair and secure them in the folds of your robe.
> (Ezekiel 5:2–3)

God's fierce judgment would soon come to pass; however, the hair tucked into Ezekiel's garment revealed there would be a glimmer of hope amongst the devastation.

More than anywhere else in Scripture, thirds are on full dis-

---

Acts 3:1 and 10:3 for more interesting happenings at this time of day.

87   Thirds in music were already mentioned for their harmony and beauty. Interestingly, there is a *diabolus in musica* or "devil's chord" in music. It is a dissonant tritone where one note is not harmonious with the other two. It communicates an unsettling, unresolved, or menacing mood.

play in Revelation.

As the angels sound their seven trumpets: A third of the earth is burned up (Revelation 8:7); a third of the sea turns to blood, a third of the sea creatures die and ships are destroyed (vv. 8–9); a star falls[88] and turns a third of the rivers and springs to wormwood (vv. 10–11); a third of the sun, moon, and stars are darkened (v. 12); and a third of humanity is killed by three plagues (Revelation 9:18).

Several chapters later, the great dragon—"the ancient serpent, who is called the Devil and Satan—" is cast out of heaven and "thrown to earth, and his angels with him" (Revelation 12:7–9). With his tail, he "swept away a third of the stars in heaven and hurled them to the earth" (Revelation 12:4). Satan brings down his corrupted demons and they "fall from heaven like a lightning flash" (Luke 10:6).

Surely, the most disheartening and mournful third in the Bible is the remnant of Israel during the end times. This will be the most terrible time in Israel's history—dwarfing even the holocaust. "How awful that day will be! There will be none like it! It will be a time of trouble for Jacob, but he will be delivered out of it" (Jeremiah 30:7). Zechariah prophecies about this day:

> In the whole land—
> this is the LORD's declaration—
> two-thirds will be cut off and die,
> but a third will be left in it.
> I will put this third through the fire;
> I will refine them as silver is refined
> and test them as gold is tested.
> They will call on My name,
> and I will answer them.
> I will say: They are My people,
> and they will say: Yahweh is our God.
> (Zechariah 13:8–9)

Though this wrath is difficult to comprehend—just as Ezekiel's

---

88   Likely a fallen angel, but that is for a different study

acting using his hair—the final note is one of hope, faith, and redemption.

7

◇◇◇◇

Perfection. Completion. Fullness.

These are archetypal messages infused into seven.

Some notable sevens in nature include: seven notes in a major scale, and seven colors in a rainbow. Interestingly, it is rather difficult to find examples of seven in nature. Perhaps because this current version of the world is not perfect?

The easiest example to find is that there are seven days in a week. Of course, we find this pattern established as God creates the world and sets it into motion.

Holy Rhythms

"In the beginning God created the heavens and the earth" (Genesis 1:1). The first sentence of the Bible is seven words in Hebrew. The first chapter works through the first six days of God beautifully and masterfully creating the universe as we know it. Then, at the beginning of chapter two, we see that:

> By the seventh day God completed His work that He had done, and He rested on the seventh day from all His work that He had done. God blessed the seventh day and declared it holy, for on it He rested from His work of creation.[89]
> (Genesis 2:1–3)

And with this consecration of the Sabbath, the Lord established a holy septuplet rhythm that would reverberate through time.

God gives His image bearers a time signature for life. John Mark Comer comments:

> *God* rested.

---

89 Note how the term "seventh day" is repeated three times, showing emphasis.

And in doing so, he built a rhythm into the DNA of creation. A tempo, a syncopated beat. God worked for six, rested for one.

When we fight this work-six-days, Sabbath-one-day rhythm, we go against the grain of the universe. And to quote the philosopher H. H. Farmer, "If you go against the grain of the universe, you get splinters."[90]

Though this seventh day is meant to be life-giving, ironically, Israel (indeed, all of us) bucked against it and there are severe splinters as a result. It speaks volumes that God would have to command something meant as a good gift (see Exodus 20:8–11; Mark 2:27; Luke 6:1–11).[91]

The Sabbath time signature was the backbeat for all of the God-appointed life rhythms of the Israelites. Every seven years was a Sabbath year. This year was to be a year of complete rest for the land. The Lord instructed the Israelites, "You are not to sow your field or prune your vineyard" and "whatever the land produces during the Sabbath year can be food for you" (Leviticus 25:1–7).

There is one more layer to this sevenfold time structure: Jubilee.

You are to count seven sabbatical years, seven times seven years, so that the time period of the seven sabbatical years amounts to 49. . . . You are to consecrate the fiftieth year and proclaim freedom in the land for all its inhabitants. It will be your Jubilee.

(Leviticus 25:8, 10; see 25:8–55 for extended passage)

To consecrate means "to treat as holy" and only the Sabbath and the Year of Jubilee receive these orders from the Lord. So, we see the "divine number" woven into a divine rule of life patterns.

---

90   John Mark Comer, *The Ruthless Elimination of Hurry* (Colorado Springs: Waterbrook, 2019) 153-54.

91   Many excellent books have been written on the Sabbath. If you are not currently observing a weekly Sabbath, I would commend this spiritual discipline to you.

God does not take neglect of His commands lightly. To not keep the Sabbath was to reject His lordship and not recognize His continual provision. The punishment was death (Exodus 31:15). Israel's failure to faithfully keep the Sabbath years is cited as the reason for their Babylonian captivity:

> Then the Chaldeans burned God's temple. They tore down Jerusalem's wall, burned down all its palaces, and destroyed all its valuable articles.
>
> He deported those who escaped from the sword to Babylon, and they became servants to him and his sons until the rise of the Persian kingdom. This fulfilled the word of the LORD through Jeremiah *and the land enjoyed its Sabbath rest* all the days of the desolation until 70 years were fulfilled.
> (2 Chronicles 36:19–21)[92]

The final holy rhythms God prescribed the Israelites were sacred festivals and holy days (see Leviticus 23). And, guess what? There are seven of them:

1. Passover
2. Unleavened Bread
3. Firstfruits
4. Feast of Weeks (Pentecost)
5. Feast of Trumpets
6. Day of Atonement
7. Feast of Tabernacles

These feasts are largely ignored in the modern church; however, buried in these traditions are incredible parallels and symbolism to mine.[93] As Paul writes, "These are a shadow of

---

92   See also Leviticus 26:27–35 for the warning God fulfilled. See Jeremiah 25:11, 29:10; Daniel 9:2 for more context.

93   To whet one's appetite for those wanting to explore more: There are many who hold the view that the spring festivals (the first four) correlate to events that have already happened and that the fall/harvest festivals (the final three) correlate to end times events.

what was to come; the substance is the Messiah" (Colossians 2:17).

Completion, Perfection

As the number seven represents perfection, it comes as no surprise that the number is prescribed by God in relation to the temple and to consecration rituals.

To ordain Aaron and his sons was a seven-day process (Leviticus 8:33–36). If a priest or the entire community of Israel sinned, part of the offering included the priest sprinkling the blood of the sacrifice seven times before the veil of the sanctuary (Leviticus 4:6, 17). On the Day of Atonement, the high priest was to sprinkle the blood of a bull seven times before the Mercy Seat (Leviticus 16:14). The purification ritual also required sprinkling blood seven times toward the tabernacle (Numbers 19:1–4). The altar itself and all the instruments used in the temple were consecrated with seven sprinkles of anointing oil (Leviticus 8:10–11).

The Lord commanded Job's unhelpful friends to present an offering of seven bulls and seven rams (Job 42:8). The offering for Pentecost included "seven unblemished male lambs a year old" (Leviticus 23:18). As David put together a grand procession to carry the ark of the covenant to Jerusalem, the Levites "with God's help. . . sacrificed seven bulls and seven rams" (1 Chronicles 15:26). After a period of wickedness in Israel, king Hezekiah reopened and cleansed the temple. With this great renewal of worship they "brought seven bulls, seven rams, seven lambs, and seven male goats as a sin offering for the kingdom, for the sanctuary, and for Judah" (2 Chronicles 29:21).

Spotting a pattern? The number seven is living up to its elevated reputation. Notice that in almost all of these previous examples, the directives come straight from God. Whatever His reasons, it is difficult to ignore His affinity for sevens.

In addition to rituals related to consecration and sacrifices, seven shows itself in both well-known and more obscure passages.

Noah is commanded to bring seven pairs of all clean animals on the ark (Genesis 7:2).

Joshua marches the people around the fortified walls of Jericho once for six days and then on the seventh day, they march seven laps around the city and have seven priests blow ram's horns (Joshua 6). With a chorus of shouts from the Israelites, God brings the walls crashing down!

Jacob bows seven times before his estranged brother, Esau, demonstrating complete respect and humility (Genesis 33:3).

When the prophet Elisha brings the Shunammite woman's son back to life, the boy sneezes seven times as his life is restored (2 Kings 4:35). The great commander, Namaan, is instructed by Elisha to wash seven times in the Jordan river to be cured of his skin disease. Reluctantly, he does and is healed and then fears Yahweh—the one true God (2 Kings 5:1–19)!

Seven is also used figuratively in poetry and other contexts.

David writes that the purity of God's Words are "like silver refined in an earthen furnace, purified seven times" (Psalm 12:6). The longest chapter in the Bible, Psalm 119, is all about delighting in God's Word. The Psalmist writes, "I praise You seven times a day for Your righteous judgments" (Psalm 119:164). In the book of Proverbs, Wisdom is personified as having a house with seven pillars (Proverbs 9:1). A most encouraging proverb is: "Though a righteous man falls seven times, he will get up" (Proverbs 24:16).

The most famous figurative example is one of Jesus' teaching moments with His disciples. It begins with Peter asking Jesus, "Lord, how many times could my brother sin against me and I forgive him? As many as seven times?" (Matthew 18:21). Jesus calls Peter's seven and raises him by 70—"70 times seven" (v. 22). This, of course, does not mean that on the 491st time you can bite the other person's head off. Jesus' subsequent parable makes the symbolic point clear: "As the Lord has forgiven you, so you must also forgive" (Colossians 3:13).[94]

We end our observation on the number seven by showcasing its eschatological appearances. The book of Revelation starts with John addressing "the seven churches in Asia" (Revelation 1:4).

---

94 As I know many people who struggle with this concept—please know that forgiveness does not mean enabling someone else's sinful behavior. It is also not the same thing as reconciliation.

The first three chapters are his seven individual letters to those churches. Revelation also depicts the completion of the Lord's judgment before ushering in the new heaven and new earth. These judgments are outlined as: seven seals, seven trumpets, and seven bowls. The threefold sevens emphasize the finality of these judgments.

Despite popular opinion, Revelation is not all doom and gloom. There are seven beatitudes, or blessing statements, woven throughout the book (Revelation 1:3; 14:13; 16:15; 19:9; 20:6; 22:7, 14). We shall conclude this section with the first of these:

> The one who reads this is blessed, and those who hear
> the words of this prophecy and keep what is written in it
> are blessed, because the time is near!
> (Revelation 1:3)

12

A powerful and authoritative number, 12 represents time or foundation.

There are twelve hours on a clock, twelve months in a year, and twelve lunar cycles in a year (which have been used in historic calendars). 12 constellations scintillate in the night sky (also referred to as *Mazzaroth* in Hebrew. See Job 38:32), which have long been used as the framework for navigation on both sea and land.

In Scripture, 12 is the bedrock in both human and heavenly establishments.

Human Infrastructure

Jacob had twelve sons. From these men come the foundational twelve tribes of Israel and the basis for almost all references to the number 12 in the Bible.

Ishmael, born to Hagar, the slave of Abraham and Sarah, was also the father of 12 great clans (Genesis 17:20). He was born out of impatience and a lapse of faith on the part of Abraham and Sarah and his descendents would be "against everyone" and "at odds with all his brothers" (Genesis 16:11–12). The Lord's pronounce-ment rings true to this day.

Joshua leads the Israelites into the Promised Land. The priests stand in the middle of the Jordan river and—in similar fashion to crossing the Red Sea—the people make their way across on dry ground (Joshua 3:17). As they take their first steps into the Promised Land, the Lord commands Joshua to have one man from each of the 12 tribes to take a stone and set them up a memorial (Joshua 4).

The temple contained many symbols representing the 12 tribes. On the shoulders of the ephod—the priestly garment— were onyx stones engraved with the names of the 12 tribes (Ex-odus 28:9–12). Likewise, the breastplate was inlaid with 12 gem-stones—one for each tribe (28:15–21). When Moses set up the tabernacle, the dedication gifts from the tribe leaders were: "12 silver dishes, 12 silver basins, and 12 gold bowls" (Numbers 7:84). The gigantic water reservoir in Solomon's temple sat on top of 12 cast oxen (1 Kings 7:24).

The bread of the Presence, 12 loaves, carefully arranged before the Lord weekly on Sabbath, were to be eaten by the priests in a holy place (Leviticus 24:5–9). As an agrarian society, these loaves were reminders that God provided their daily bread. Ultimately, the Lord's presence is the foundation of life. Jesus says, "I am the bread of life" and now all believers, the true "royal priesthood," find our sustenance in Him (John 6:35; 1 Peter 2:9).

Jesus built His ministry around 12 disciples.[95] Jesus accom-plished His ministry, set the groundwork for the church, and changed the entire world through His chosen Twelve.

Our final look at 12 in the physical realm of Scripture inter-sects with our previously explored number seven. Twice, Jesus miraculously feeds large crowds (see Matthew 14:13–21; 15:32–39).[96] Both times, He takes bread and fish, gives thanks, and all the people eat and are satisfied. So, why did the disciples gather 12 baskets full of leftover bread the first time and seven "large bas-kets" full the second time (Matthew 14:20; Matthew 15:37)? The

---

95 He also had an inner circle of three disciples—Peter, James, and John—and a larger group of 70 (Luke 10:1).

96 The numbers 5,000 and 4,000 in these passages are only counting the men. The numbers were easily twice that many when including the women and children.

answer is in the audience. The first crowd is Jewish and would have immediately recognized the meaning of the number 12 in the miracle they had just experienced. The second crowd was Gentile. The larger type of basket used[97] and the number seven show that Jesus' perfect gift of life "is God's power for salvation to everyone who believes, first to the Jew, and also to the Greek" (Romans 1:16).

Heavenly Infrastructure

The number 12 symbolically shows up in the spiritual realm as well.

Jesus tells His disciples that "In the Messianic Age, when the Son of Man sits on His glorious throne, you who have followed Me will also sit on 12 thrones, judging the 12 tribes of Israel" (Matthew 19:28). After Peter hacks off the ear of the high priest's slave, Jesus rebukes Him and adds, "Do you think that I cannot call on My Father, and He will provide Me at once with more than 12 legions of angels?" (Matthew 26:52–53).

In Revelation, John describes his vision of the New Jerusalem, bright and beautiful, descending out of heaven:

> The city had a massive high wall, with 12 gates. Twelve angels were at the gates; the names of the 12 tribes of Israel's sons were inscribed on the gates. There were three gates on the east, three gates on the north, three gates on the south, and three gates on the west. The city wall had 12 foundations, and the 12 names of the Lamb's 12 apostles were on the foundations.

> The one who spoke with me had a gold measuring rod to measure the city, its gates, and its wall. The city is laid out in a square; its length and width are the same. He measured the city with the rod at 12,000 stadia. Its length, width, and height are equal.
> (Revelation 21:12–16)[98]

---

97 The Greek word here is the same used when Paul makes his dumbwaiter-style escape out of Damascus (Acts 9:25).

98 A *stadion* is about 600 feet. Therefore, 12,000 *stadia* is ~1,400 miles. For context, Alaska is about 1,400 miles from north to south. The International Space

Whether or not these measurements are to be interpreted literally, the depiction fits perfectly with the archetypal meanings of 12. This awe-inspiring city is part of the New Heaven and New Earth all followers of Jesus look forward to.

40

It is all downhill from here!

40 is not generally considered a "nice" number. 40 represents testing and trials, yet also transition.

The word "quarantine" originates during the bubonic plague where infected persons were told to stay isolated for 40 days. A typical pregnancy is 40 weeks—which can be trying but is also a beautiful transition to the birth of new life and parenthood. Monopoly—a game likely responsible for more family feuds than any other—has 40 spaces around the board. (Coincidence? I think not!)

Let's explore this daunting number in Scripture and see what we can learn.

Trials, Tribulations, Testing

In the wicked days of Noah we encounter our first 40. Once Noah finishes building the ark just as God had commanded, God gives him a week's notice that the floodwaters are imminent: "Seven days from now I will make it rain on the earth 40 days and 40 nights, and I will wipe off from the face of the earth every living thing I have made" (Genesis 7:4). The number 40 is mentioned six times during the account of this great calamity that remodeled both landscape and life.

Israel's times of trials are marked by 40 as well. Most notably, they were destined to wander in the wilderness for 40 years before entering the Promised Land due to their sin. The Lord's verdict: "You will bear the consequences of your sins 40 years based on the number of the 40 days that you scouted the land, a year for each day. You will know My displeasure" (Numbers 14:34).

Station orbits 248 miles above the earth.

One of Israel's most vexing enemies—the Philistines—are associated with periods of 40. For 40 days, the giant Goliath would stand and taunt Saul and the Israelite army before a young David, through the power of the Lord, slayed him (1 Samuel 17:16). During the time of Samson, Israel acted wickedly and "so the Lord handed them over to the Philistines 40 years" (Judges 13:1).

The ministries of Moses, Elijah, and Jesus were marked by periods of 40 days. Moses communed with Yahweh on top of mount Sinai for 40 days and 40 nights (twice) and did not eat or drink (Exodus 34:28).[99] Elijah, while fleeing the evil Jezebel, received a divine food delivery and "on the strength from that food, he walked 40 days and 40 nights to Horeb, the mountain of God" (1 Kings 19:8).

Jesus' ministry was bookended by 40-day stretches. After His baptism, Jesus was led by the Spirit into the wilderness to be tested by the Devil and He fasted for 40 days and nights (Matthew 4:2; Luke 4:2). Jesus, Elijah, and Moses are the only ones in Scripture to have no food or water for 40 days (all three appear together during the Transfiguration. See Matthew 17). After His resurrection, Jesus stayed 40 days showing Himself alive to many people and teaching before His ascension (Acts 1:3). This was the transitional period before Pentecost—the beginning of what we call the "Church Age" in which we are currently living.

While these times of testing and trials can be challenging, God still shows mercy and provision through them all. Whether it is an ark, manna, or the power of His Word, we can have confidence in the Lord through all tribulations and transitions.

Chronos & Kairos

Prophetic Weeks

There is another species of numbers that I believe every believer should study the nature of and, at the very least, be acquainted

---

99   Moses' life can also be seen in three forty-year sections. He was forty when he killed an Egyptian who was mistreating a Hebrew (Acts 7:23). He was eighty years old when God called him through the burning bush and he and Aaron spoke to Pharaoh (Exodus 7:7; Acts 7:30). And Moses died at the age of 120 (Deuteronomy 34:7).

with. Specifically, we shall look at prophetic weeks and their related numbers. We begin with one of the most astounding prophecies in all of the Bible.

More than five centuries before the birth of Christ, Daniel receives a message from the angel Gabriel. Within this message are these words:

> Know and understand this:
> From the issuing of the decree
> to restore and rebuild Jerusalem
> until Messiah the Prince
> will be seven weeks and 62 weeks.
> It will be rebuilt with a plaza and a moat,
> but in difficult times.
> (Daniel 9:25)

These "weeks" are prophetic weeks. Each week equals seven years.

It's time to do some math.

The Jews followed a lunar calendar of 360-day years. Therefore, 69 (7 weeks plus 62 weeks) seven-year weeks would equal 483 years or 173,880 days.

The decree issued by king Artaxerxes to allow Nehemiah to go back to Jerusalem and rebuild the wall was in 444 BC (most scholars say Nisan 1, to be exact). Fast-forward 173,880 days and where do we land? At the triumphal entry of Jesus into Jerusalem.[100]

Gabriel is delivering this word to Daniel over 500 years before the birth of Jesus—how astounding!

Incredibly, this message also prophesied that Jesus would die (Daniel 9:26). Information on the end times is also contained in these verses. This guides us to one last prophetic number. . .

Forty-two months—1,260 days. Time, times, and half a time.

It goes by many names, but three and a half years is a consistently prophetic length of time. For example, the prophet Elijah prayed and it did not rain on the land for three years and six months (1 Kings 17–19; Luke 4:25; James 5:17). It is also half of a

---

100   Scholars put this at Nisan 10, A.D. 33. Others say it lines up with the crucifixion. Either way, it is within those few days. Simply amazing!

full prophetic week (Daniel 9:27).

In Revelation, this number appears six times in chapters 11–13. These echo prophecies through Daniel speaking of "time, times, and half a time" (Revelation 7:25; 12:7).

The two witnesses empowered by God will prophesy for 1,260 days (Revelation 11:3). When they are slain by the beast (the antichrist), their bodies lie unburied in public "And representatives from the peoples, tribes, languages, and nations will view their bodies for three and a half days and not permit their bodies to be put into a tomb" (v. 9). After these three and a half days, the Lord resurrects them and they are caught "up to heaven in a cloud, while their enemies watched them" (v. 12).

The woman with "a crown of 12 stars on her head" (notice one of the numbers we explored. The woman is interpreted as Israel) is persecuted by the beast. But God enables her escape to the wilderness where He sustains her for 1,260 days, or "a time, times, and half a time" (Revelation 12:6, 14).

Finally, we find that "the nations" are allowed to "trample the holy city for 42 months" (Revelation 11:2). Also, for forty-two months, the beast is allowed to wage war and rule (Revelation 13:5). These two terrible time periods are the same length as the other references of three and a half years; however, they are differentiated in months.

What are we to think of all these things? It is beyond the scope of this chapter to get into the tribulation, the timing of events, and exacting eschatological interpretations. Nevertheless, these prophetic weeks and numbers point straight to the sovereignty of God. The two witnesses are empowered by God (Revelation 11:3). The woman goes to a place "prepared by God" (Revelation 12:6). And the beast has only as much authority as is "given" by God (Revelation 13:5). We know who wins the final battle! What God pronounces will always come to pass.

Matchless Math

In Greek, there are different words for various concepts of time.

Chronos refers to the general, sequential, quantitative passage of time. It is the unrelenting current of ticking seconds. An example is: "It is not for you to know times [chronos] or periods that the Father has set by his own authority" (Acts 1:7).

Kairos is qualitative and refers to a specific, opportune moment in time. It is a crescendo bursting forth in the musical score of time. "For while we were still helpless, at the right time [kairos], Christ died for the ungodly" (Romans 5:6).

Yahweh is the creator, sustainer, and governor of chronos and kairos. He holds time in His hands and everything happens at its appointed moment.

There are some "numbers" we cannot know—the number of our earthly days or the date Christ shall return—but seeing the patterns He does give us should bolster our faith. We see these prophetic fulfillments and, in turn, we are not to worry about the numbers out of our control. Instead, trust Him. Trust His perfect timing.

The Lord "does great and unsearchable things, wonders without number" (Job 5:9). "He brings out the starry host by number; He calls all of them by name. Because of His great power and strength, not one of them is missing" (Isaiah 40:26).

> God, how difficult Your thoughts are
> for me to comprehend;
> how vast their sum is!
> If I counted them,
> they would outnumber the grains of sand;
> when I wake up, I am still with You.
> (Psalm 139:17–18)

How wonderful that God—the One who spoke numbers, equations, and time itself into existence—loves us! He counts the number of hairs on your head (Luke 12:7). In His grace He "would count [our] steps but would not take note of [our] sin" (Job 14:16). Jesus was counted among the outlaws so that we could be counted in the resurrection to new life (Isaiah 53:12; Luke 22:37). Yes, "where sin multiplied, grace multiplied even more" (Romans 5:20).

He has set eternity in the human heart (Ecclesiastes 3:11) and we will praise Him from everlasting to everlasting (Psalm 106:48). "To Him be the glory both now and to the day of eternity" (2 Peter 3:18).

9

Remember

Prone to wander, Lord, I feel it;
Prone to leave the God I love:
Take my heart, oh, take and seal it
With Thy Spirit from above.

Robert Robinson, AD 1758

Keep looking up. . . that's the secret of life

Snoopy

One could argue that this final adventure is the intention of all the preceding symbols.

This is to abide in the vine; to bask in His light; to drink of the Living Water; to embrace sanctifying fire; to commune with our spiritual family together with our Abba; to walk in His freedom; to find our identity in His "names" for us; and to find comfort and confidence in His designs and sovereignty.

Our hearts are frustratingly prone to wander—to forget all of these truths. This is, however, nothing new. From the Israelites to the apostles, there is much wisdom to glean about remembering.

Ebenezers

We humans have a peculiar aptitude for amnesia when it comes to God's continual presence and faithfulness.

We are forgetful people. But God knows this and He provides us with reminders.

A glance at all of the God-given rituals and rhythms of life for the Israelites will reveal a common theme—remembering.

An excellent example of this is the Lord's commands related to trumpets:

> When you enter into battle in your land against an adversary who is attacking you, sound short blasts on the trumpets, and you will be remembered before the LORD your God and be delivered from your enemies. You are to sound the trumpets over your burnt offerings and your fellowship sacrifices and on your joyous occasions, your appointed festivals, and the beginning of each of your months. They will serve as a reminder for you before your God: I am Yahweh your God.
> (Numbers 10:9–10)

The Lord enveloped the Israelites with reminders. The fourth commandment was to "remember the Sabbath day, to keep it holy" (Exodus 20:8). Part of the meaning of this weekly ceasing was to remind the Israelites that they had been slaves in Egypt and that God had rescued them "with a strong hand and an outstretched arm" (Deuteronomy 5:15). The Lord instructed that blue-corded tassels that were to be sewn onto the corners of garments. He explains their purpose:

> Tassels for you to look at, so that you may remember all the LORD's commands and obey them and not become unfaithful by following your own heart and your own eyes. This way you will remember and obey all My commands and be holy to your God.
> (Numbers 15:38–40)

More reminders were embedded into the priestly attire and duties. In the sacrifices continually offered up, there was the reminder of sins (Hebrews 10:3). The jewel-studded breastplate with the names of the tribes was to be worn by the priest "as a continual reminder before the LORD" (Exodus 28:29). The atonement money collected from the people for the operation of the tent of meeting was considered a "ransom" to remind the Israelites to atone for their lives (Exodus 30:11–16). These are but a sampling of the rich reminders God threaded into Israelite society.

Believers today are no longer under the law. But this, of course, does not mean we do not require reminders. Thankfully, the church has many facets to help us remember who we are and Whose we are.

Just as the societal rhythms were done in community, the church is a community. Within this family, we are to remind one another of God's truth and grace. Paul writes, "Let the message about the Messiah dwell richly among you, teaching and admonishing one another in all wisdom, and singing psalms, hymns, and spiritual songs, with gratitude in your hearts to God" (Colossians 3:16). We are to continually point one another to the Head of the church—Christ.

Though we may have lots of knowledge of the truth (sometimes especially then), we need encouragement. Peter writes, "I will always remind you about these things, even though you know them and are established in the truth you have" (2 Peter 1:12). Paul reminds Timothy "to keep ablaze the gift of God" that is in him (2 Timothy 1:6). Look around at your brothers and sisters in

Christ. All of them are testimonies and reminders of God's amazing grace.

There are two sacraments observed by the church that serve as beautiful reminders: Baptism and the Lord's Supper. Though our own baptism is a single event, every time a new family member is baptized, we rejoice for them and with them! As we observe others identifying with Christ through baptism, we are reminded of our own baptism and true identity.

As a church family, the Lord's Supper is regularly observed. The Lord instructed, "Do this in remembrance of Me" (Luke 22:19; 1 Corinthians 11:23–26). We are reminded of our sin, our incalculable debt, paid in full by the precious blood of the Lamb. We are reminded of the communion we can now have with God through our great High Priest. And we are reminded that Jesus will return, "for as often as [we] eat this bread and drink the cup, [we] proclaim the Lord's death until He comes" (1 Corinthians 11:26).

Not all reminders for the Israelites were directives from the Lord. Many times, an altar or marker would be built as a memorial of what God had done in that place. Commonly, the Israelites would take the most permanent item they could get their hands on—stone—and construct a monument. (Some examples include: Deuteronomy 27:1–8; Joshua 4; 24:24–28.) One such memorial was built by Samuel, who "took a stone and set it upright between Mizpah and Shen. He named it Ebenezer" (1 Samuel 7:12). The name Ebenezer means "Stone of Help."

We can construct our own stones of remembrance in our lives. These Ebenezers mark miracles, events, or milestones of the Lord's extraordinary grace. As with the Israelites, these may also represent a period of transition. Perhaps it is our moment of saving faith or when God rescued us out of a season of "slavery" or "wandering through the wilderness." Certainly, we do not want to unnecessarily dwell in the past. Rather, it should keep us humble and grateful as it reminds us of the incredible kindness of God. When facing new challenges, we remember His past faithfulness. We rest in His unfailing love.

With all of these reminders, know that the Lord is unchanging and has always kept His word. Yes, "He remembers His covenant forever, the promise He ordained for a thousand generations" (Psalm 105:8). From rainbows to resurrection, Yahweh perfectly fulfills every one of His promises.

Through it all, remember that He is *with* you. Jesus gave His promise that He would not leave us as orphans (John 14:18). True to His word, we have the Holy Spirit with us and *in* us! He is the One of whom Jesus said, "[He] will teach you all things and *remind* you of everything I have told you" (John 14:26). He will never leave or forsake us. Assuredly, "He who started a good work in you will carry it on to completion until the day of Christ Jesus" (Philippians 1:6). May we be encouraged and remember He is with us always, to the end of the age (Matthew 28:20).

Remember to Look Up!

With all the reminders around us, may we not simply look, but truly "taste and see that the LORD is good" (Psalm 34:8). Look at the trees outside, look at the falling rain, look at the rays of sunlight piercing the clouds—be reminded. Perceive, ponder, and let it prompt us to truthful thoughts and loving deeds.

And how can we remember what we do not know in the first place? We cannot meditate on that of which we are unaware. How can we speak the truth in love to ourselves or others if we do not read and listen to the Voice of Truth? How can we teach others His ways (Psalm 51:13), if we do not follow them ourselves? Through these reminders, "let us strive to know the LORD" (Hosea 6:3)! Doctor Martyn Lloyd-Jones says it well: "You must go on to remind yourself of God—who God is, and what God is, and what God has done, and what God has pledged Himself to do."[101]

Ironically, remembering the Lord will lead to a humble self-forgetfulness. We can be so myopic in our selfishness. We look inward for guidance and look down on others instead of upward to the Light and outward that we may extend love. As C.S. Lewis put it, "To love and admire anything outside yourself is to take one step away from utter spiritual ruin".[102]

---

101   D. Martyn Lloyd-Jones, *Spiritual Depression: Its Causes and Cures*, (Grand Rapids: Wm. B. Eerdmans Publishing Co., 1965), 20-21.
102   C. S. Lewis, *Mere Christianity*, (New York: Harper Collins), 127.

As mentioned in the introduction, one of the goals of these themes is to come to a place of awe—an awe of God that explodes into worship. And worship "is humble and glad, worship forgets itself in remembering God; worship celebrates the truth as God's truth, not its own".[103] Worship is loving God. Love is not the opposite of hate. Love is the opposite of selfishness.

So, lift up your heads! Look! Look at the Lord who is love.

Look at Christ Jesus—remembering the gospel.

Just as Moses lifted up the bronze snake in the wilderness and those Israelites who looked to it were cured, so Jesus was lifted up "so that everyone who believes in Him will have eternal life (Numbers 21:4–9; John 3:14–15). The Lord raised up the righteous Branch of David on that cursed tree, "But the One God raised up did not decay" (Jeremiah 23:5; Acts 13:37; Psalm 16:10). No, He was "lifted up from the earth" to draw all people to Himself (John 12:32). And believers can say, "God raised up the Lord and will also raise us up by His power" (1 Corinthians 6:14). We are raised to a new life and a blessed hope!

The conversion testimony of the great English preacher, Charles Spurgeon, is a witness to our theme:

> The minister did not come that morning; he was snowed up, I suppose. At last a very thin-looking man, a shoe-maker, or tailor, or something of that sort, went up into the pulpit to preach. Now it is well that preachers be instructed, but this man was really stupid. He was obliged to stick to his text, for the simple reason that he had little else to say. The text was—"LOOK UNTO ME, AND BE YE SAVED, ALL THE ENDS OF THE EARTH" (Isaiah 45:22)
>
> He did not even pronounce the words rightly, but that did not matter. There was, I thought, a glimmer of hope for me in that text. . .
>
> The preacher began thus: "This is a very simple text indeed. It says 'Look.' Now lookin' don't take a deal of pain.

---

103   N. T. Wright, *For All God's Worth: True Worship and the Calling of the Church* (Grand Rapids, MI: Wm. B. Eerdmans Publishing Company, 2014).

It ain't liftin' your foot or your finger; it is just 'Look.' Well, a man needn't go to College to learn to look. You may be the biggest fool, and yet you can look. A man needn't be worth a thousand a year to look. Anyone can look; even a child can look. . .

Then he looked at me under the gallery, and I daresay with so few present, he knew me to be a stranger. . . . Then lifting up his hands, he shouted, as only a Primitive Methodist could do, "Young man, look to Jesus Christ. Look! Look! Look! You have nothing to do but look and live!"

I saw at once the way of salvation. I know not what else he said—I did not take much notice of it—I was so possessed with that one thought. . . . I had been waiting to do fifty things, but when I heard that word, "Look!" what a charming word it seemed to me. Oh! I looked until I could almost have looked my eyes away.[104]

Oh, "Those who look to Him are radiant with joy; their faces will never be ashamed" (Psalm 34:5). And once we have looked, let us "fix our gaze straight ahead," keeping "our eyes on Jesus, the source and perfecter of our faith (Proverbs 4:25; Hebrews 12:2).

Look intently into the gospel—the perfect law of freedom— as we run the race with endurance (James 1:25). We "have been raised with Christ" so now we "seek the things above, where Christ is, seated at the right hand of God." Setting our "minds on things above, not on earthly things" (Colossians 3:1–2). He will keep us from straying to the right or to the left as we journey from sanctification to glorification.

Our glorious hope will not disappoint and is not far off. "Lift up your heads, because your redemption is near!" (Luke 21:28). We long for this day and with Job we say,

---

104   Apparently, Spurgeon told this story over 280 times in his preaching career (https://www.christianitytoday.com/history/issues/issue-29/spurgeons-conversion.html).

But I know my living Redeemer,
and He will stand on the dust at last.
Even after my skin has been destroyed,
yet I will see God in my flesh.
I will see Him myself;
my eyes will look at Him, and not as a stranger.
My heart longs within me.
(Job 19:25–27)

So, we keep looking and remembering until we behold Yahweh with our own eyes. For He tells us, "I will create a new heaven and a new earth; the past events will not be remembered or come to mind" (Isa. 65:17).

"Look!" says the One seated on the throne, "I am making everything new" (Revelation 21:5).

II

All Things Made New

10

All Things Made New

". . . thus they will love, and reign in love, and in that godlike joy that is its blessed fruit, such as eye hath not seen, nor ear heard, nor hath ever entered into the heart of man in this world to conceive; and thus in the full sunlight of the throne, enraptured with joys that are forever increasing, and yet forever full, they shall live and reign with God and Christ forever and ever!"

Jonathan Edwards, Heaven: A World of Love

"The gospel is far greater than most of us imagine. It isn't just good news for us—it's good news for animals, plants, stars, and planets. It's good news for the sky above and the earth below."

Randy Alcorn, Heaven

In the introduction, it was hinted that there is a single section of Scripture where all of these thematic explorations come together. This passage dictated the symbols chosen for this book because of this very fact. While there are many more amazing symbolic themes throughout the Bible (horns, donkeys, rocks, bread, etc), the decision was made to narrow the focus with this one passage in mind.

I have decided to include it in its entirety here.

Its position in Scripture is equally fascinating: It is the final chapter of the Bible. . . Revelation 22:

> Then he showed me the river of living water, sparkling like crystal, flowing from the throne of God and of the Lamb down the middle of the broad street of the city. The tree of life was on both sides of the river, bearing 12 kinds of fruit, producing its fruit every month. The leaves of the tree are for healing the nations, and there will no longer be any curse. The throne of God and of the Lamb will be in the city, and His slaves will serve Him. They will see His face, and His name will be on their foreheads. Night will no longer exist, and people will not need lamplight or sunlight, because the Lord God will give them light. And they will reign forever and ever.

> Then he said to me, "These words are faithful and true. And the Lord, the God of the spirits of the prophets, has sent His angel to show His slaves what must quickly take place."

> "Look, I am coming quickly! The one who keeps the prophetic words of this book is blessed."

> I, John, am the one who heard and saw these things. When I heard and saw them, I fell down to worship at the feet of the angel who had shown them to me. But he said to me, "Don't do that! I am a fellow slave with you, your brothers the prophets, and those who keep the words of this book. Worship God." He also said to me, "Don't seal

the prophetic words of this book, because the time is near. Let the unrighteous go on in unrighteousness; let the filthy go on being made filthy; let the righteous go on in righteousness; and let the holy go on being made holy."

"Look! I am coming quickly, and My reward is with Me to repay each person according to what he has done. I am the Alpha and the Omega, the First and the Last, the Beginning and the End.

"Blessed are those who wash their robes, so that they may have the right to the tree of life and may enter the city by the gates. Outside are the dogs, the sorcerers, the sexually immoral, the murderers, the idolaters, and everyone who loves and practices lying.

"I, Jesus, have sent My angel to attest these things to you for the churches. I am the Root and the Offspring of David, the Bright Morning Star."

Both the Spirit and the bride say, "Come!" Anyone who hears should say, "Come!" And the one who is thirsty should come. Whoever desires should take the living water as a gift.

I testify to everyone who hears the prophetic words of this book: If anyone adds to them, God will add to him the plagues that are written in this book. And if anyone takes away from the words of this prophetic book, God will take away his share of the tree of life and the holy city, written in this book.

He who testifies about these things says, "Yes, I am coming quickly."

Amen! Come, Lord Jesus!

The grace of the Lord Jesus be with all the saints. Amen.

Beyond Words

This is the grand finale of all things.

In Revelation, the word "like" is used over fifty times. Most of those instances are an astonished John attempting to describe what he is seeing in his visions. He sees "something like a sea of glass mixed with fire" (Revelation 15:2) or hears a "loud voice like a roaring lion" (Revelation 10:3). He cannot quite put them into words. It is beyond words.

But "like" does not make an appearance in chapter 22.

John does not say he saw something "like a tree of life." No, he saw *the* tree of life. John does not say they will "see something like God's face." No, he writes that they *will see His face*.

To truly ponder this is beyond words.

This does not mean that symbolism is absent in this passage (e.g., Jesus is not actually a star). However, the lack of "like" communicates a certain unambiguity—a definitiveness that we can stake our hope and faith on. A future that is true yet, in many ways, is incomprehensibly amazing.

We shall attempt to put some of what we do know through Scripture into words, but they must fall utterly short of our destined reality. This is the redeemed universe all of creation has been groaning for. This is the place where all of our thematic threads lead.

Redemption Realized

Though our faith may have only been the size of a mustard seed, we will see and enjoy the everlasting life it grew into. Through grace by faith, the saints shall see and experience that faithful and true are the words of the One who is called Faithful and True (Revelation 22:6; 19:11).

"Hope deferred makes the heart sick, but a longing fulfilled is a tree of life" (Proverbs 13:12). And what do we see in Revelation 22? The tree of life. All of our longings, our dreams, our deepest desires will be answered with new, abundant life.

In Revelation 22, God continues to exercise His masterful creativity. But instead of a garden, we behold a grand city. No tree of

Good and Evil in this place—only the Tree of Life. Its fruit is born in and out of season. In fact, it is not restrained by seasons; the fruit ripens every month wreathed by healing leaves that will not wither.

There will be no thorns or thistles or painful labor. Cultivation shall be free from the curse. We will uncover the ability to be fruitful in all we do. There will be no weeds cropping up in the gardens of our resurrection reality and no enemy planting unwanted seeds. Harvests will always be abundant—in our work and our relationships. All of it sustained by our absolute abiding in the Root of David.

We shall have the ability to bear unblemished spiritual fruit—a consummate cornucopia of love, joy, peace, patience, kindness, goodness, gentleness, faithfulness, and self-control. Being fruitful will be our state of being. The labor pains—to which humans and all creation were subjected—have ceased. Through the labors of Christ—conquering sin and death—new life is born.

Just imagine: What sort of work—unhindered by all real and metaphorical thorns and thistles—will we individually and collectively accomplish for our good and to the glory of God? As Adam worked alongside God to name the animals, we will once again be intimate coworkers with the Lord.

The people of God "did not take the land by their sword—their arm did not bring them victory—but by Your right hand, Your arm, and the *light of Your face,* for You were pleased with them" (Psalm 44:33). Though the Lord dwells "in unapproachable light," we will be able to approach Him! Nations will come to His light and to His radiance (see Isaiah 60:3).

Night will no longer exist (Revelation 22:5). The dark days of our sorrow will be over (Isaiah 60:20). No more will there be wandering in physical, mental, emotional, or spiritual darkness. There will be no more attempts to cover ourselves in darkness to hide our shame and fallenness. There will be no more struggle of spiritual refraction where we used to imperfectly reflect the Divine Light—now only undimmed and unhindered basking in His majestic brilliance.

We will see His face. Tears well up reading it. With unveiled, renewed eyes, we gaze upon His glory. No longer will "we see indistinctly, as in a mirror," but "face to face" (1 Corinthians 13:12). Our faith will be made sight.

Shining brighter and brighter, no substrate will subtract from our reflecting the image of the Heavenly Man as we should (Proverbs 4:18; 1 Corinthians 15:49). His divine light will enable us to see Him and others clearly, and will guide us on right paths forever.

The river of living water scintillates in the divine light and is crystal clear; nothing shall ever pollute these waters. Never again will our souls ache with any unquenchable thirst.

The streams of living water within us will have fully sprung forth into eternal life (John 4:14). We will have arrived at the Fountainhead.

> There in heaven this fountain of love, this eternal three in one, is set open without any obstacle to hinder access to it. There this glorious God is manifested and shines forth in full glory, in beams of love; there the fountain overflows in streams and rivers of love and delight, enough for all to drink at, and to swim in, yea, so as to overflow the world as it were with a deluge of love.[105]

The living water is a gift. As it flows "from the throne of God and of the Lamb," it will never run dry.

The flaming, whirling sword guarding paradise has been removed! We will freely take the fruit from the tree of life. There will be no fire of tribulations; only the zealous flames of the one true living God. Our souls will be warmed by the heat of His fiery, jealous love.

In amazement, we will observe the cherubim and seraphim. We will resonate with their chorus of: "Holy, holy, holy is the LORD of Hosts" (Isaiah 6:3). Indeed, His glory will fill the new heaven and earth and set our hearts ablaze in awe.

The bride of Christ will commune forever with her Groom in a marriage that will never divorce—a marriage that will remain faithful and true because it is with the One who is Faithful and True. No sanctuary is to be found in the New Jerusalem, for the

---

105   Jonathan Edwards, *Heaven: A world of Love.*

Lord and the Lamb are its sanctuary (Revelation 21:22) and He will tabernacle with His people forevermore. It is the happily-ever-after union our hearts have truly desired. The church and Christ growing in oneness in a great mystery which parallels the Trinity. As the Groom, Christ will pursue each one of our hearts—not only chase after, but every time catch and captivate. The central provocation of Solomon's chiasm will ring true as we feast and are indelibly intoxicated with the love of Yahweh (Song of Songs 5:1).

We will experience freedom in Christ in full. The deceiver, the one who accuses believers and questions our identity, is vanquished. The serpent's head is crushed! We will no longer be slaves to sin with the utter inability to do that which we know is good and right—always finding that evil is right there with us. The inner-self war raging between what we ought to do and our fleshly desires. . . gone! And it is replaced now with freedom. Perfect freedom. Fulfilled freedom.

We, His slaves, will serve God (Revelation 22:3). As we joyfully serve, what new and incredible things shall be in store for all of us in the new heaven and earth? It is the glory of God to conceal a matter and for man to uncover it (Proverbs 25:2). Perhaps God will hide discoveries simply for the pure joy of watching His people discover them—like parents watching children excitedly unwrapping Christmas presents.

Our identities in our new reality will be in line with who we are meant to be in Christ. No idols will ever again supplant the Lord in our hearts and minds. Strivings shall cease and that "God-shaped void" in our hearts—the one that inclined us toward idolatry and that led to so much heartache—will be filled with endless contentment. The Lord's Name will be on our foreheads—we are His, and our identities will find *shalom* in Him.

The tree of life produces its twelve kinds of fruit every month. But how exactly will time work in the new heaven and earth? What happens to the fundamental equations of physics when timelessness is applied? What use will counting be when the important things of that future reality are immeasurable? It is a mystery. But the mortal must be clothed with immortality in order that we may participate in timeless communion with our infinite, heavenly Father.

No longer will we require "reminders." For what we had to remember on the old earth will become our reality. Forgetfulness of God will be forgotten. Our senses will never dull. Rather, they will be perfectly attuned to take in all the wonders that shall surround us.

We will drink the fruit of the vine anew with Jesus in heaven, just as He promised (Matthew 26:29). There will be a splendid celebration of the great gospel truths—those truths angels desire to look into—with an always overflowing, never diminishing sense of gratitude and joy.

The previous things—including all our sins—will have passed away. "For I will create a new heaven and a new earth; the past events will not be remembered or come to mind" (Isaiah 65:17). The Lord says, "It is I who sweep away your transgressions for My own sake and remember your sins no more" (Isaiah 43:25). Yes, God "will cast all our sins into the depths of the sea" (Micah 7:19). And when the "first heaven and the first earth had passed away. . . the sea no longer existed" (Revelation 21:1).

Incredibly, the Lord will forget our sins, *yet also* remember any and all of our righteous acts.

> Every kingdom work, whether publicly performed or privately endeavored, partakes of the kingdom's imperishable character. Every honest intention, every stumbling word of witness, every resistance of temptation, every motion of repentance, every gesture of concern, every routine engagement, every motion of worship, every struggle towards obedience, every mumbled prayer, everything, literally, which flows out of our faith-relationship with the Ever-Living One, will find its place in the ever-living heavenly order.[106]

Jesus told His disciples, "Whoever gives just a cup of cold water to one of these little ones . . . I assure you: He will never lose his reward!" (Matthew 10:42). Store up for yourselves treasures in heaven! He says, "Look! I am coming quickly, and My reward

---

106   Bruce Milne, *The Message of Heaven and Hell* (Downers Grove, Ill: InterVarsity, 2002), 257.

is with Me to repay each person according to what he has done" (Revelation 22:12). How unfathomably gracious our God is!

Oh, believer, may you not be able to unsee these reminders in creation directing the gaze of our hearts to our Creator. May they be an aid in remembering these truths until the day we know them in full.

Observe the trees and remember to abide that you may bear much fruit. Feel the sun warm your face and remember you have an inheritance in the Light of Life. Take a sip of cool water and remember you have springs of eternal Living Water within you. Light the stovetop or fireplace and remember to fan the flame that is within you in holiness and passion for Christ. Look at family and marriage and remember our grand heavenly union with the Lord our God. Make a purchase, and remember your freedom in Christ and the price that was paid. Sign your name, and remember Christ's defining declarations over your identity. Check the time, and remember God's sovereignty and faithful love that is the same today, yesterday, and forevermore.

Look. Pay attention. Remember. And let it lead you to upward-directed awe.

Looking back from the other side—that is, if we even desire or are capable—we shall see every thread of creation, history, and of our lives was woven together with His love. Peace that suprasses all understanding will now be our constant state. We will have reached the harbor we longed for (Psalm 107:30).

Amen! Maranatha!

From Him and through Him and to Him are all things.
(Romans 11:36)

Soli Deo Gloria

Acknowledgments

That this book even came to fruition is a miracle and gift from the Lord. This is coming from the guy that procrastinated on every paper in high school. The credit for the funding to edit, publish, and market this book is to God's provision and perfect timing.

I'm so very grateful to all of my VIP readers who took time to give me invaluable feedback on the manuscript.

Thank you Carl Dobrowolski, president of Goodwill Media (GoodwillMediaServices.com) for your wisdom, guidance, and gift of encouragement. Special thanks to my superlative editor, Jim Holmes (greatwriting.org). I admire your discernment, skill, and care. Much gratitude to Chris Powers (fullofeyes.com) for your gift of artistry and making the vision for the cover come to life. My parents are continually conduits of the Lord's good grace in my life. I am blessed beyond words to be their son. If this book had too much alliteration for you, you may thank (or blame) my mother.

My beautiful bride, Michelle, has been a constant source of support. You are a gift of pure grace—I love you. Our kids have granted (and continue to grant) me new perspectives on the love of our heavenly Father. From Him and to Him and through Him are all things.

About the Author

Benjamin Marshall is the founder of Ignite Media—a company designed to fan the flames of love in believers for the Lord and His Word. He is a member of the Summit Church and a leader in the Faith Driven Entrepreneur network. He is honored to be the husband of Michelle and stepdad to Oliver, Henry, Charlotte, and William. He and his family live in Apex, North Carolina. Feel free to reach out at to him at this address:

Benjamin@ignitemedia.press

About the Cover Art

When Ben asked me to create the cover art for *The Invisible Clearly Seen*, I was initially hesitant. I don't typically take on commissions. However, I was intrigued by the way he tethered each chapter so closely to the climactic vision of the Apocalypse (Revelation 22:1-5), a passage to which I have also given much consideration. Ultimately, the chance to "visually exegete" this passage and tie that together with the themes of Ben's book was enough to convince me to see what I could do. The cover art, then, serves as a visual exegesis of Revelation 22:1-5 and simultaneously (I hope) functions as a single eidetic summation for the main themes addressed in this book.

Chapter one addresses garden and horticultural symbolism; this is reflected in the double "tree of life" referenced in Rev.22:2, by which the New Jerusalem is cast in decidedly Edenic hues.

Chapter two looks at light and shadow imagery, pictured here in the slain and risen Jesus Christ who, as the radiance of the glory of the unseen God, is the light of the new creation (Rev. 21:23).

The waters of chapter three appear in the crystal river flowing from the throne as an echo of the waters that pour from the side of the Pierced Christ of John 19:34, who is also the eschatological temple of Ezekiel.

The fiery passion of chapter four appears in the seven flames surrounding the Bride, which are the seven spirits (i.e., the sevenfold Spirit) of God by whom the Church is united in love to Christ.

The blood of chapter five is pictured here as binding God's people to Himself in Christ and washing the Bride white as snow.

The seal that marks God's people for Himself, as considered in chapter six, is pictured in the five wounds of Christ above the Bride's head which—illumined by the light of resurrection—have become jewels in her nuptial crown.

Chapter seven's emphasis on names is suggested in the Bride's turning toward her Lord, such that her identity is found in beholding (because first beheld by) Him.

Chapter eight's discussion of numbers finds expression in the (hyper) cube of the New Jerusalem whose foundation is the cruciform radiance shining from the face of the slain and risen Jesus.

The entire picture serves to support chapter nine's call to remember. And the final chapter is, again, summarized in the image as a whole which grasps at a depiction of the "all things new" achieved through Jesus' death and resurrection.

Any artistic representation falls woefully short of the glories that begin to unfold themselves before us in these final chapters of John's Apocalypse. However, my hope is that this image, paired with Ben's book, might help us to taste—even a bit more clearly—the wonders of a reality founded upon, sustained by, and moving inexorably toward the crucified and risen Lord.

Christopher Powers | Full of Eyes